"A must read for anyone who cares about social justice and healing racism."
—Cherie R. Brown, founder and executive director,
National Coalition Building Institute

"An invaluable contribution to the oral history of the impact of racism on all Americans."
—Derek Douglas, vice president for civic engagement,
University of Chicago

"Heartbreaking and heartwarming—devastating in . . . scope and specificity, but uplifting in demonstrating how people have overcome not only their own prejudices but also those of friends and family."
—Katrina vanden Heuvel, editor and publisher of *The Nation*
and author of *The Change I Believe In*

"The first step toward healing is to realize that we're all in this together. *Combined Destinies* puts this in perspective like no other book. Read it and let one more false dichotomy dissolve into a deeper understanding of the way forward."
—Van Jones, former special advisor to the Obama
White House and author of *Rebuild the Dream*

"This is a powerful collection that challenges us all to think about the role of race in our lives and our communities—and helps us do that. . . . This book highlights just how important these continuing conversations about race are—for every person, of every race, of every background."
—Cecile Richards, president,
Planned Parenthood Federation of America

"This book provides a rare vision for engaging in a lifetime of work with ourselves, each other, community, and society. Wherever you are on your journey in confronting racism, you will find this book to be a gift of love."
—Rea Carey, executive director,
National Gay and Lesbian Task Force

"[This book] is also about the influence racism has on those whose lives are touched by and intersect with whites. . . . This book moved me to tears. . . . When we create space for soul-revealing storytelling, we also create windows of opportunity to transform lives and reclaim souls from the damaging impacts of oppression."
—Larry D. Roper, professor of ethnic studies
and vice provost for student affairs, Oregon State University

"For all of us on the road to social change, we must first learn to walk on the bridge to a multicultural America. *Combined Destinies* is part of that path, excavating our pasts through personal accounts but also pointing forward."
—Larry Cohen, president, Communication Workers of America

"Invites truth telling, reflection, and learning with compassion and empathy."
—Karen V. Hansen, professor of sociology and women's
and gender studies, Brandeis University

"Courageous and personal testimonials present powerful evidence that all humanity, regardless of race or ethnicity, is victimized by racism. More important, the book demonstrates that many individuals have pursued a path that leads to a place of honesty, sharing, acceptance, and understanding."
—Patrick Gaston, president, Western Union Foundation

"With grace, passion, and authenticity, *Combined Destinies* reveals the long-hidden story of how racism harms whites too. These stories, full of grief but also inspiration, show us how to heal the wounds that racism has caused."
—James Forman Jr., clinical professor of law, Yale Law School

"Elegantly interweaves the stories of contributors with the editors' commentary, which provides perceptive and wise context."
—Patrice Vecchione, author of *Writing and the Spiritual Life:
Finding Your Voice by Looking Within*

COMBINED DESTINIES

COMBINED DESTINIES

WHITES SHARING GRIEF ABOUT RACISM

Edited by Ann Todd Jealous and Caroline T. Haskell

Foreword by
Julian Bond and Pam Horowitz

POTOMAC BOOKS
An imprint of the University of Nebraska Press

Excerpts from Debra Busman's "You Gotta Be Ready for Some Serious Truth to Be Spoken,"
an excerpt from *Fire and Ink: An Anthology of Social Action Writing*, eds. Frances Payne Adler,
Debra Busman, and Diana Garcia (Tucson: University of Arizona Press, 2009), 3–6, originally
published in *Social Justice: Pedagogies for Social Change* 29, no. 4 (2002): 150–52. www.socialjustice
journal.org, reprinted by permission of the author and the University of Arizona Press.

Library of Congress Cataloging-in-Publication Data
Combined destinies: whites sharing grief about racism / edited by Ann Todd Jealous and
Caroline T. Haskell; foreword by Julian Bond and Pam Horowitz.
pages   cm
Originally published: Washington, D.C.: Potomac Books, c2013.
ISBN 978-1-61234-695-3 (pbk.: alk. paper) 1. Racism—United States—Psychological aspects.
2. United States—Race relations—Psychological aspects. 3. Whites—United States—Attitudes.
4. Race awareness—United States. I. Jealous, Ann Todd. II. Haskell, Caroline T.
E184.A1C573 2014
305.800973—dc23
2014008392

For our fathers with deep gratitude.
Their capacity for love far outweighed their social conditioning.

Racism is . . . a negation of the deepest identity of the human being, who is a person created in the image and likeness of God.

Pope John Paul, 1997

In order for us, black and white, to disenthrall ourselves from the harshest slave master, racism, we must disinter our buried history.

Studs Terkel, 1992

Contents

Acknowledgments

We have gratitude for the clients, friends, and family members whose shared grief about racism and resistance to racist conditioning inspired this endeavor. We thank the contributors to this anthology for their courageous willingness to break through years of silence. Without their stories, this book could not have been written.

We are eternally grateful to Fred Jealous and Gary Fujii, whose unwavering support, encouragement, and love sustained us throughout the years we worked on this project. We are deeply appreciative of Mamie Todd and Virginia Wilder for their careful reading, maternal love, and certainty of the importance of this effort. We thank Lara Jealous who gave us invaluable feedback in the book's initial stages and served as its midwife by introducing us to Dana Newman, our dedicated and hardworking agent to whom we are greatly indebted. Our thanks, also, to Fran Baca and Connie Bauer, whose feedback early on was very helpful. We are appreciative of Benjamin Jealous's consistent and valuable support. We are grateful for the innumerable friends who questioned us about this anthology. Each time we were able to talk about it was easier than the last.

We thank Hilary Claggett, our Potomac Books editor, whose enthusiasm for this project elicited her own stories, thus affirming our strong belief in its value. We are indebted to Martin Luther King Jr. for the title, which was inspired by a passage from his "Letter from a Birmingham Jail" (Alabama, 1963): "Injustice anywhere is a threat to justice everywhere. We are caught in an inescapable network of mutuality, tied in a single garment of destiny. Whatever affects one directly, affects all indirectly." We especially thank those of you who will allow these stories and the Reader's Guide to inspire self-reflection and the beginning or continuance of conversations related to the universal damage created by racism.

Foreword

*Julian Bond and Pam Horowitz**

JB & PH: It is fitting that we first learned that this book was being written at a screening of Tate Taylor's *The Help* (2011). Adapted from a novel by Kathryn Stockett and set in 1960s Mississippi, the movie told a story of the relationship between whites and the black maids who served them—and who raised their children. It is a fictionalized version of a story told in this book's opening chapter by a woman whose name is Anne. She writes of the lifelong loss she felt when the black woman who "had been [her] mother in another life" was banished from her home without explanation or even a chance to say good-bye.

The Help struck the same theme as this book: racism inflicts pain on its practitioners as well as its victims. The movie, while imperfect, made audiences, black and white, weep and cheer.

This book will have a similar effect on its readers, each of whom will be the better for it—just as those whose stories are told "expressed gratitude for the opportunity." As one put it, "Thank you for giving these thoughts a voice."

JB: Deborah (chapter 4) writes, "There were no spaces in my white world, no openings whatsoever, to talk, think, or feel about race. . . . There was no discussion of race, racism, or white dominance in my K-12 schooling

---

*Julian Bond, chairman emeritus of the National Association for the Advancement of Colored People (NAACP), and Pam Horowitz, a lawyer, live in Washington, D.C.

experiences or my university experience." Deborah is an adult reflecting on her youth, but too often whites growing up today still find few spaces "to talk, think, or feel about race."

At the University of Virginia, where I have taught for the past twenty years, white students in my seminar on "The Black and White Sixties" wanted their class sessions to serve as group therapy where they could explore their feelings and experiences surrounding race because they had no other outlet for such discussions.

PH: At least these white students were attuned to issues of race. If you ask white people how racism impacts their lives, too many would say it does not. I grew up largely in racial isolation; but my Jewish father and gentile mother knew prejudice firsthand, and that saved me from total ignorance and insensitivity. Ironically, it didn't stop me from bullying a fellow classmate—because of her religion. Walking with a friend behind Carol one day on the way to school, when we were probably nine years old, we started to taunt her about being a Jehovah's Witness. Of course, we didn't know what that meant, just that it was different and that made Carol different. We kept this up for about a block until Carol sat down on a stoop and began to sob. We were mortified and apologized profusely. I learned right then one of the lessons Liz (chapter 3) learned: "We cannot inflict pain on others without hurting ourselves in the process."

JB & PH: This book teaches many lessons, not the least being that "even when individual white people are not actively perpetuating mistreatment, they continue to remain part of an invisible system of racism that maintains their privilege at the expense of people of color."

As the historian John Hope Franklin wrote a few years before his death:

> *All* whites . . . benefited from American slavery. *All* blacks had no rights they could claim as their own. *All* whites, including the vast majority who owned no slaves, were not only encouraged but authorized to exercise dominion over *all* slaves, thereby adding to the system of control. . . .

Most living Americans do have a connection with slavery. They have inherited the preferential advantage, if they are white, and the loathsome disadvantage, if they are black, and these positions are virtually as alive today as they were in the nineteenth century.*

Two hundred forty-six years of slavery were followed by a hundred years of state-sanctioned discrimination, reinforced by public and private terror, ending only after a protracted struggle in 1965.

Some now ask us to believe that no permanent damage was done to the oppressors or the oppressed. Some ask us to believe that we Americans are now a healed and whole people.

This book tells a different truth.

PH: Ann Jealous, Caroline Haskell, and I each married a man of a different race or ethnicity. As Fred (chapter 2) writes, "Part of marrying into an African American family is to be intimately exposed to the pain of racism on an ongoing basis and to marvel at all of the victories so many African Americans have achieved in the face of death and unrelenting life threatening, humiliating, and vicious obstacles."

Only one generation stands between Julian Bond and human bondage. His grandfather and great-grandmother were property, like a horse or a chair. Whenever I hear the story of the white people who owned them, I am filled with shame. At age fifteen, barely able to read or write, Julian's grandfather James hitched his tuition—a steer—to a rope and walked a hundred miles across Kentucky to Berea College, from which he graduated fourteen years later. Whenever I hear James's story, I am profoundly humbled.

JB & PH: In 1968, the year he was killed, Martin Luther King Jr. spoke about the successes and failures of the modern civil rights movement:

While this period represented the frontal attack on the doctrine and practice of white supremacy, it did not defeat the monster

---

* John Hope Franklin, Letter to *The Chronicle*, Duke University student paper (May 2001).

of racism. If we are to see what is wrong we will have to face the fact that America has been and continues to be largely a racist society. And the roots of racism are very deep in this country. . . . Racism is a faith, a form of idolatry; it is the dogma that one ethnic group is condemned to eternal inferiority and another ethnic group is somehow given the status of eternal superiority. It is not based on anyone going out and studying the facts and then coming back out of it and saying that as a result of experimental studies that these people are behind because of environmental conditions. Racism is based on ontological affirmation. It is the contention that the very being of a people is inferior. And the ultimate logic of racism is genocide. . . . It is the ultimate arrogance of saying God made a creative error. This is the evilness of racism.

King was speaking approximately 350 years after racism (i.e., white supremacy) was introduced to these shores, and more than forty years ago, but he might as well have been speaking today.

Racism is the subordination of people based on skin color. It is a self-perpetuating system of advantage based on race. It is prejudice plus power. White supremacy is the ideology that justifies white domination. Martin Luther King described it as a faith, a form of idolatry.

We think of racism in terms of individual behavior and individual actions, but it is a complex set of societal actions and attitudes. There are two kinds of racist behavior, active and passive. They are conscious and unconscious, and each provides benefits, both material and psychological, to its practitioners.

For all their years in the United States, black people and other people of color have struggled with the existence of racism and the questions it raises. White people must join in this struggle, as they do in this book, if we are to overcome.

This book doesn't preach. It doesn't lecture. It tells stories. Read them.

And weep.

And cheer.

Preface

Ann Todd Jealous

When I returned from my fiftieth high school reunion, I decided to act on a long-standing thought that an anthology of stories about the impact of racism on the lives of white children, women, and men could make an important contribution to the literature of anti-oppression work and to individual and societal healing. I want to introduce you to this book by telling you how that decision came to be.

In 1955, when I was fourteen years old, I enrolled in a historically white high school with nine other African American students, most of whom were my friends. It was the year that the state of Maryland was forced to honor the Supreme Court's decision to desegregate public schools. I was intent on getting the best education possible, and I believed that it was important to do whatever I could to support the effort toward equal treatment of all Americans. Since its inception in 1844, this public school had an excellent academic reputation, only female students, and many graduates among its teachers, giving it a better-than-average chance of empowering adolescent girls. Until that day, however, I had almost no contact with white people.

I have many negative memories connected to the three years that I spent at Western High School. During the first year, being intentionally tripped on the stairwell and pushed against walls was a common occurrence, and I still have a vivid memory of being surrounded by a group of white girls in the lunchroom, an organized attempt to prevent me from sitting down to eat my lunch. As time passed, some of my white classmates became very friendly, but such interactions were totally restricted to school activities, to the point of my not being acknowledged if I saw them on the street with their parents.

My most meaningful memories of racism are related to the actions of adults. We were given seat assignments on the front rows in our various classes to assure that the teachers could watch "the Negro girls"; the assumption was that we would cheat if we were left unmonitored. I had a seat near the window in one class that first year, and I remember looking out at the mothers of other students picketing the school in protest of our presence. In my junior year, the school newspaper staff chose me to represent the school in a statewide newswriting competition. That year, the principal refused to allow the school to continue its long-standing tradition of participating in that contest.

One day the American history teacher, a woman who had spent much of her life in Georgia, home to many of the Creek and Cherokee people, announced to the class, "We've already done too much for the American Indian." Angered by what I believed to be a blatant lie and recognizing the power that she had to negatively influence the thinking of so many students with her racist opinion, I took hour-long bus rides to the Library of Congress each week for most of that semester to do research that I hoped would prove her wrong. I was disappointed by the dearth of books by Native American authors and allies but gratified to have found one small way of resisting the racism that was so rampant among the adults in that school. It was clear to me that because of her position of authority, her statement had the potential of being far more damaging to prospects for social equality than any of the racist behaviors of individual students.

I was a sensitive adolescent, and I spent a great deal of effort consciously and intentionally teaching myself to dissociate from my feelings as I went through each day so that anxiety and emotional pain would not interfere with academic progress. In addition to dealing with my own experiences of racial abuse, it was stressful to witness the ways in which school personnel treated my African American classmates and friends and to realize that I had no power to change their abusive behavior. I also made a decision to withhold most of the details of my school life from my parents and other adult family members because they had to deal with their own hurtful experiences of racism on a daily basis, and I wanted to protect them from mine. On one occasion, though, when the guidance counselor refused to mail my applications to predominantly white colleges and universities that interested me, I did ask my mother to intervene.

Despite the reality of eventually having several positive high school experiences and one supportive English teacher, I primarily felt tremendous relief upon graduation. I had no desire to see that school again.

Fifty years later, in 2008, I was living on the other side of the country. The Internet was active, and it was possible to find almost anyone—even those of us who didn't want to be found. One day, an e-mail arrived from a white high school classmate whose name I didn't remember. She was helping to organize the fiftieth high school reunion. There would be a luncheon and a presentation about our high school years, and she wanted me to come.

After much deliberation and a few disturbing dreams, I realized that I needed to return to the school in order to put the past to rest. Looking forward to seeing at least some of the African American women who shared the high school experience with me and for whom I still felt great fondness, I boarded a plane bound for Baltimore.

There were two surprises at that luncheon. I learned that several of my African American classmates had attended every reunion in order "to hold a place for us." I was proud of them, proud of their determination, proud that their memories of discrimination and attempted intimidation had not interfered with that decision.

The other surprise came from a white woman who spoke to me about a comment I'd made fifty-two years before when we were fifteen or sixteen years old—one which had greatly informed her life decisions. We were standing in a small group during a recess from classes, she said, and having recently entered the school as a junior and newly experiencing classes with black students, she made a "racial comment." Then, realizing that I was there and that I might have been offended, she apologized to me. I responded by quietly saying, "It's okay. I'm used to it." My comment and the shame she felt upon recognizing that she had just played an active part in a hurtful system gave her great pause, she said, and set the basis for her becoming a minister and raising her children in an atmosphere of racial tolerance and interracial friendship.

Later, as I reflected on that brief conversation and on that afternoon's program, it occurred to me that my white schoolmates had also been hurt by the racism that created intense separation, and the restriction of cross-racial friendships to school grounds also deprived them of the richness that cultural diversity brings to relationships. I wondered how the shame and guilt others may have carried because of racist words and behaviors had affected their lives. Perhaps, as adolescents, some of them had also been confused by the double standards that, once removed from the constraints of bigotry, made no sense. The distress of the adults in our lives—our teachers, counselors, parents—and their inability to help any of us effectively deal with the physical and emotional situations we were in was largely a consequence of the lack of racial diversity in their own lives and the ignorance and fear that come from living with sameness.

That conversation was only one in a series of experiences that has allowed me to realize how badly white people have been hurt by the system of racial oppression. It has taken many years, many conversations, and deep work on my own healing. It has also taken witnessing the release of enormous grief during my work as a psychotherapist and diversity trainer. Despite the availability of courses in multiculturalism and workshops in diversity training, and despite the increase in relationships of various kinds across racial lines, most white people seem to be unaware of the emotional price they pay for even unwanted participation in such a system.

Although racial oppression certainly includes prejudice (i.e., prejudgment), hurting someone's feelings through unfair and discriminatory treatment, and being mean-spirited to someone of a different race, it is not the same as any one or even any combination of those characteristics. "Racism"—the belief that one race is intrinsically superior to others and the behavior stemming from that belief—is about power. When we talk about racism, we are talking about white supremacy as an institutionalized system of economic and social oppression of one group of people by another. It is based on skin color and/or racial identification, it only goes from the politically dominant group to the racial minority group, and it is always actively and/or passively socially sanctioned.

There have always been Americans of European heritage who have fought for human equality and justice out of their own conscious recognition that a system of racial oppression is a prison we are all caught in, regardless of whether we are in a dominant or subdominant position. The first white person I ever met, read, or heard of whom I really believed understood that all Americans are hurt by racism was Lillian Smith, a writer and dedicated social critic of the segregated South. Spending an hour with her in 1960 immediately after reading *Killers of the Dream*, her most influential book, was life changing for me.

When I shared tales of my reunion experience and my desire to take on this project with my friend and colleague, Caroline Haskell, she agreed to be coeditor. As we conducted interviews and received stories, we discovered common emotional threads—shame, sadness, confusion, despair, and guilt—all of them indicators of grief and/or trauma. Like Lillian Smith, we have no doubt that the social evil called racism—a system of oppression that was created long before any of us were born—has made us all its victims. Unless we all do whatever we can to eradicate it, racism will continue to undermine human decency and goodwill.

Introduction

Caroline T. Haskell

When Ann asked me if I would consider working with her on this project, I was overwhelmed. Feelings of excitement, anxiety, trepidation, and nervousness flooded through me, and this huge, looming doubt appeared. Could I do this? Was I up to the task? Why had Ann picked me? The more my feelings seemed to overtake me, the more sure I became of my answer. Even though Ann had graciously told me I could think about it, I looked at her and said, "Yes, I will. I need and want to work on this book with you." So, I jumped in!

I think my emotional reaction to working on a book about the impact of racism on white people is similar to some of the feelings many white people have whenever the subject of racism is raised. Discomfort, fear, dread, and a huge desire to get away from the conversation are common reactions. Racism is a deeply emotional topic, producing feelings of shame, guilt, embarrassment, and grief. One of the ways in which white people have been impacted by racism is the conditioning against wanting to look at or address the feelings that we are uncomfortable with. How often have I tried to escape and avoid these feelings? We have been trained not to want to examine ourselves and the system in which we participate. The premise of this book, though, is to do just that. How have we, as white people, been damaged and hurt by the very system that we (our people) created? For we did not escape being deeply affected by racism, although the ways in which we have been hurt differ significantly from the ways in which people of color have been oppressed.

I have been involved in anti-oppression work for almost thirty years. Initially, largely due to some awareness I had about the privilege I had been born into, I chose a career in the helping professions, to be of service to others. As my understanding deepened, I realized that being of service to others served me as well. I began working in earnest on myself, committing to honest self-examination, recognizing that my privilege had come at a cost to my own humanity, to my ability to be fully human, and I did not want to keep paying that price. This work included reading about racism, reaching out to people of color, and developing relationships. I asked a lot of questions, both about the experiences of people of color in this country and about myself. I developed a fearlessness in asking people of color whom I trusted how they experienced me as a white person. And I learned to lower my defenses and truly hear what they had to say. I learned to stay open, rather than closing myself off. This work is an ongoing and life-long process.

The pull to avoid my feelings is enormous. I struggle to keep my conversation connected with my heart, when I would rather run away to the distant comfort of an intellectual and rational approach to racism. Racism is not rational, so intellectualizing discussions about it is not helpful. And still, although the insight is there, the emotional challenge remains! I have to face myself, heart wide open and vulnerable to the feelings that show up. Repressing my feelings cuts me off from myself and other people, and it stunts my development as a human being. I sometimes catch myself pretending, pretending that I am "okay," that I have not been affected by the damage that racism causes.

It is clear to me that no amount of trying to figure it out with my head is going to get me where I need to be. This confusion, this emotional block toward understanding and the subsequent desire to stop looking at it is one example of how my racist conditioning has hurt me. Another way I have been damaged by racism is the tendency to think that I don't need to understand what people of color are trying to get me to see. My husband, a Japanese American man, will sometimes observe that I seem unable to grasp something he is talking about, even when I want to understand. Fortunately, there are people in my life who are also committed to my growth and development as a whole person.

Since Ann and I are working on this project together, Ann often asks me questions that keep me looking at my own conditioning around race. She holds me accountable for this self-examination. She believes in my capacity to continue to learn and change. I consider the opportunity to work on this book with Ann as part of my life-long journey to reclaim myself and help other white people do the same.

My hope, in the creation of this book, is to extend an invitation to my white brothers and sisters to join this conversation, to add your voices to those contained here, and to commit to healing the wounds of racism in your own lives.

1 Separation from Caregivers and Family Members

Without words, it comes. And suddenly, sharply, one is aware of being separated from every person on one's earth and every object, and from the beginning of things and from the future and even a little, from one's self. A moment before one was happily playing; the world was round and friendly. Now at one's feet there are chasms that had been invisible until this moment. And one knows, and never remembers how it was learned, that there will always be chasms, and across the chasms will always be those one loves.

Lillian Smith, *The Journey*

One of the most distressing consequences of racism is enforced separation from loved ones without an emotionally safe place to express grief or a caring person with whom to share it. When we are unable to find the space where we can freely mourn our losses, there is no release. Without release, there is no healing. It is as though grief freezes, and, regardless of whether we deny its existence or are painfully aware of it, its weight becomes a burden that will manifest itself in ways that may lead to addiction or physical illness or to patterns of thinking and behaving that interfere with the health of all our relationships. If we are afraid of receiving negative sanctions for the outward expression of our grief, we either swallow it and hurt ourselves or act it out as anger and hurt others. Out of our pain, we may make decisions that will negatively affect us for the rest of our lives.

As is true for many white Americans, Anne formed a deep childhood bond with an African American woman who was hired by her parents to care for their home and their children. Her memories include the delight of eating cool watermelon on hot summer days with Essie, her beloved caregiver. As a child, Anne had no awareness that racist caricatures and other ludicrous images of African Americans eating her favorite fruit were flooding the world of art in the U.S southland, adding to senseless and humiliating stereotypes. She only knew the pleasure of sharing a delicious and healthy food with a dearly loved friend. One day, she came home from school to discover that Essie was gone. There had been no warning and no explanation was offered. Anne was not able to heal from that profound loss until she was well into adulthood.

This is Anne's story:

My first memories are of Essie. She started working for my parents long before I was born. My parents married during World War II. After it ended, they built a house on Shades Mountain (near Birmingham, Alabama). Eight-year-old Sandy and four-year-old Billy, my father's children, came to live with them. My mother and father were jewelers and they both chose to work long hours.

My earliest memories are of Essie dressing me in the back hall over the floor heater. It was warm there, and I would sit in her lap and she would hold my feet out over the heater to warm them. Essie smelled really good. Even now, the smell of certain face powder reminds me of her. Essie was a short woman; she called herself "stout." Her arms and legs were slender but strong. She was beautiful. It's funny what my mind remembers about Essie. She could scrub the entire floor by hand, leaning over and not bending her knees.

I remember waiting at the window for Essie to arrive each morning. She rode the bus from her home in Oak Grove. Since I knew the sounds that the bus made, I could anticipate her arrival. I loved that bus for bringing her in the morning and hated it for taking her away in the afternoon. I needed her to stay with me. It never occurred to me that she had three children of her own also waiting for her to come home. I remember screaming and holding onto her clothes, not wanting her to go. I felt so afraid and alone at night. She would have protected me from the bad things that happened. She put my well-being above everything else. But she had to go home, and that left me alone. I would have gone home with her every night if I could have.

Sometimes, I would ride the bus with Essie in the afternoon when my mother would work late. Essie would bring me downtown to meet my parents where they worked. It always confused me when I would ask Essie to sit up front on the bus and she would say no. Essie very seldom refused me anything, and that puzzled me for a long time. When I was old enough to realize why Essie had to sit in the back of the bus, I was indignant. I would sit in the back with her, and I would glare at the other white people as if I wasn't one. I think I felt a cosmic responsibility for Essie. I took on the guilt of all the white people that had hurt my Essie. Even today, I instinctively trust black people more and am more comfortable with them than with others.

In the summers, we would go to the beach for a week. The restaurant owners wouldn't let Essie eat with us or even use the restrooms. I would refuse to go into the restrooms if Essie couldn't. We would pee behind the building and eat in the car or under a tree. The trip to the beach was terrible, but after we got there things were fine. Vacations were especially nice because Essie didn't go home at night. Sometimes, she would even sleep with me.

We shared a great love for watermelon. Once, when we were at the beach, we went out for dinner, and, of course, Essie had to stay home. That night, I begged my parents for a watermelon to take home for Essie. When we got home, I found out that Essie had walked a great distance to a store to buy a watermelon for me and had carried it all the way back to the house. We laughed and ate watermelon together all week.

There was no doubt in my mind that Essie loved me and no doubt in her mind that I loved her. I think she had been my mother in another life and came back to finish the job. Or maybe she was an angel sent to help me survive my childhood. Whatever she was, she was the most kind, loving woman in my life, and I will love her forever.

Recently, I was listening to a newscast about an allegation of racial profiling, and the woman admitted that she "was just afraid of black people." I realized that I have had just the opposite feeling. If I had to choose between two strangers to trust and one was a person of color and the other wasn't, I would choose the person of color as most likely being the safe one. I find myself still feeling this way. Actually, I have never had that instinct be wrong for me. Interesting. Thank you, Essie.

Children who witness abuse are generally powerless to effectively intervene. Thus, they too are its victims. This is as true for racial abuse as it is for other forms of physical, sexual, emotional, and spiritual abuse. The impact of witnessing racial abuse is most profound when the targeted victim is someone whom the child loves.

Although Brenda grew up in South African apartheid, geographically distant from Anne's Alabama childhood, her story and the grief she experienced with the sudden and unexpected separation from her primary caregiver is dramatically similar to Anne's.

Brenda writes:

Just under the surface of my white skin I was always itchy. Like a pernicious rash, the condition never went away and would often worsen, erupting into outbursts of anger and sorrow that I could not explain. I constantly felt ashamed of my parents' behavior, and, above all, of myself. I never did understand why I was not able, as I was so often told to do, to "just behave" myself!

My family was not well-to-do; in fact, they went bankrupt the year I left home, but like almost every white family in mid-twentieth century South Africa, we had several domestic servants. My parents routinely left home early and returned late, fully preoccupied with the challenge of running a small business that perennially ran into debt. However, there were always servants around our house: One woman to work in the kitchen and clean house, and another woman who was the nanny, taking care of us, three girls and a boy, each five years apart. My parents also employed a man who did heavy housekeeping and yard work. And on Mondays and Tuesdays another woman came to our house to do the washing, an enterprise so convoluted that I can still remember each detail of "Wash Day."

My relationship to these servants was very complicated. On the one hand, there was no question that they, as adults, were in charge and would frequently give us orders. On the other hand, I knew that even little me, at age six, in some odd way was entitled to boss them around. We called the servants by first names, while simultaneously being taught that when children addressed adults we must use a term of respect. When we were speaking in Afrikaans, we also needed to use the formal pronoun. This was indeed tricky! The white neighbor whom we seldom saw was addressed as "Miss Vorster," while on the other side of our fence lived "Tannie [Auntie] Watkins." We called our parents' friends aunt or uncle, regardless of family relationship, yet the servants only had first names.

I was maybe nine or ten years old when I realized that the servants' names were not their real names at all. I found it both fascinating and repelling that these human beings had their names assigned in the same way that we named our pets, the mongrel Fluffy and my beloved collie dog, Laddie. So in our house we had Dora, Lily, Martha, Rebecca—all white people's names, easy to pronounce and to remember.

No black person was accorded the dignity of a last name, of some family name to indicate relatives, parents, or children, just like us. Even my Granny's servant, who worked for our family for over twenty-five years, was only "Alina."

So I asked questions. As would happen time and again, I found there were no answers. The servants told me to go away and let them get on with their work. My parents pretended to not understand what I was asking, or to scold me for being "too big for my boots." My father even coined a nickname for me. He called me Little Miss Bigboots, often reminding me that I was only a pip-squeak, and some things were just not children's business. I bitterly resented being dismissed like this and eventually learned to hide my questions and to suppress the welter of emotions. Names became inextricable from respect and dignity, and, when I could not solve the tangle, became yet another persistent irritant under my skin. No wonder I itched so much!

I was not always conscious that my skin was white and my eyes blue. Thinking back to my littlest self, I know that warmth seeped into my skin from the round brown woman called Dora. I must have been quite small, small enough for Dora to tie me onto her back with a blanket. My cocoon smelled like Dora, and as I chaffed my cheeks against the rough-woven blanket, I knew I was safe there. When I was four years old, I suffered a severe attack of gastro-enteritis. I don't know how long I was sick, but Dora was always there with me, comforting, cleaning, soothing me. Later I heard my parents lying about my recovery, saying that a German nurse had found the cure to save my life. I was left speechless, furious, knowing it had been Dora.

Indeed, I had proof that Dora would always keep me safe. I went once with my mother and grandmother to the beach in Durban. Dora accompanied us on the same train, although she had to travel in the third class and could not come to see us on the long journey. The first time I saw ocean and waves I was spellbound with their movement. In great excitement, I ran into the water without any idea what might happen. In short order, I was knocked down by a wave, tumbling over and over. I was thrashing around, terrified and choking, unable to breathe, when Dora pulled me out and held me tight. Once I calmed down, I saw that her clothes were all wet.

Even then I knew that she could not find a changing-room. I was sorry that she had to stay in her wet clothes, but I feared even more that she would get into trouble because the signs on the beach-front—Net Blankes/Whites Only— meant that black people must not go in the water where white people went swimming. I already knew that bad things happened to black people because when the police came to our neighborhood there would be sirens and shouting. Later, when it was quiet again, I could hear crying. With a child's belief in magic, I hoped with all my heart that those signs did not apply to Dora. After all, she was more brown than black.

The whole question of skin color bewildered me. Dora was brown and our cook, Lily, was nearly black, while Alina was like some of the tanned white people on the beach. I examined my own skin closely, putting my arm or hand beside a piece of paper to see how white I was. I remained perplexed and unconvinced. My skin looked more orange or pinkish. How could anyone tell? Also, I had many brown freckles, like my mother and sisters. Did that count? Yet more mystifying was that I had never seen anyone the color of my crayon called "Flesh" in my big box of twenty-four Crayola crayons. This was another itchy question, one more that my parents would not answer.

Then, one day, Dora left. I did not know that she was going and she did not say goodbye. Dora was just not there anymore. I felt sure that I had done something so naughty, so evil, that Dora had gotten very angry and left. Then again, I wondered if I had made her break the law so that she had to go to jail. Shame and guilt made my skin hot and itchy. I cried and cried. When my parents punished me for crying, I cried even more. I felt feverish and afraid without Dora, furious at my mother who, I became convinced, had been the one to send Dora away.

With time I developed a hypersensitive wariness, a feeling that my dearest relationships exist in an active earthquake fault zone where forces beyond my control might at any moment shatter everyone dear to me and blow my world apart. In that diabolical system of identifications and separations that lay at the core of Apartheid by the enforcement of laws whose specific intent was the spurious division of humanity, love and compassion were generally excluded.

I never learned why Dora left. What I did learn, indelibly, was that people, especially those people I love, cannot be trusted and will someday leave me.

With each successive loss and betrayal, I insulated myself from grief, trusting less and less. With time, accumulated experience grew into belief. Even now, though Apartheid's odious laws pass into history, I continue to testify that among millions, I remain collateral damage.

Bonnie's love for her African American nanny and the despair that accompanied their enforced separation has informed her entire life.

This is Bonnie's story:

To this day I cannot tell you what Mamie looked like, nor do I have any pictures to show you. However, in my heart and soul, I experience her as my birth mother.

My dad was a functional alcoholic who joined the secret service during World War II and returned a changed, damaged man. My mom, one of twins, was subservient to her stronger and sometimes abusive sister. She had an obsessive-compulsive personality and learned to control her obsessions and hide her anger by pretending to be weak and sweet. She couldn't function as a homemaker, and we always had maids, cooks, and laundresses. More than anyone else, Mamie seemed to be there for me.

I believe that my night feedings as an infant couldn't be counted on, that crying was soon abandoned, and that there was just the waiting for Mamie. I felt as though I was on solid ground when Mamie held me; I was afraid of being dropped when I was in my mother's arms. My mother's arms were fragile and insubstantial; Mamie's arms meant joy, stability, and returned love. Mamie was my looking-glass self. She mirrored approval, hope, and unconditional kindness.

When I was three years old, the family moved from South Shore Chicago to Cincinnati. Mom, Dad, and my brothers, ten-year-old Bill and eight-year-old Bob, moved. I came soon thereafter on a train with my aunt. Mamie stayed in Chicago.

During that train ride, I wandered off from my aunt and I remember her finding me in the lap of a round, soft black woman. I repeated this action and I was once again forcefully taken back to our seats and given a tongue-lashing. To this day, the connection one has to walk through from train car to train car scares me and brings to mind this little caper of my three-year-old self.

When in Cincinnati I was uncontrollable. I felt lost, angry, and abandoned. I remember feeling sickened by my mother, the white woman who was trying to take care of me. Once during my tirades, I was sent to my room. I sat on my bed and threw one marble after another at my door. The dining room from which I had been banished was below my bedroom. Some large figure came into the room and hands hit me across the face, sending me flying across the room. My head hit against the wall and all went black. From then on, I learned to deep freeze my emotions. I have a picture of myself at that time. I am standing between my brothers and there is a vacant look on my face.

Once when I was a little older, I asked for "Mamie's spaghetti" and Bill came at me with a can of Franco American and shouted and spelled the words out to me: "'Franco American'; not Mamie's." I felt robbed and couldn't remember why it was Mamie's to me in the first place.

When we were young adults, Bob and I were involved in civil rights. Embroiled in and supportive of black power, I remember pondering over my nineteen-year-old face in the bathroom mirror, rubbing the skin of my face and examining the roots of my hair. I was perplexed that my complexion was beige. Beige. It just couldn't be. I worked in South Stockton. My friends were black. It came as a shocking revelation that the color of the skin on my face was not the same as that on Mamie's face. I had drawn so much sense of myself and such stable and vibrant love from her that I believed we looked the same. My face was white. What color was my soul?

My father died when I was thirty-six and my mother died when I was thirty-eight. With both parents gone, I recovered memories in my sleep at night. Memories of their neglect, their drinking, and the loneliness that I especially felt after my youngest brother left home. I realized that I had not been allowed to live my life unless I was also caring for my mother. These memories were like a spotlight exposing parts of my life I had worked so hard to repress. I spent years in a hypervigilant mode of shock, trauma, and depression.

My love for my parents is conflicted. For Mamie, my love and grief are simple and unfettered. I miss and yearn for her to this day. If only I had never had to leave her. She gave me the firm foundation from which to gather the shards of my soul. Studying for a master's degree in child development taught me the importance of those early years. I am very thankful for the unconditional love that I received from Mamie.

Since I believe that loving thoughts and thankfulness extend beyond this short life, I also believe that she knows that I love her for all she did for me yesterday, for the genuine longing that I have for her today, and for the future she helped me pass on to my daughters.

A child in need of love does not look at skin color but at the genuineness of love returned.

The strong connection between racial oppression and economic oppression has been well researched. Maren's childhood story is an excellent example of an experience common to children and grandchildren of wealthy white people who employ people of color to serve them.

These are Maren's memories:

My first awareness of color differences occurred through my father occasionally driving our "cleaning woman," Odessa, home to Seaside. She was African American, as were her neighbors. My dad made a point of telling us that this was "where the black people live." The way he said it made it seem like another country and sort of scary, yet I was intrigued.

Odessa's daughter, Linda, was just a little older than I. She sometimes came to our house with Odessa, and we became friends. She was my only non-Caucasian friend for many years, as my family lived in a very white neighborhood and my schools were the same.

I got a combined dose of racism and classism from my grandmother. She and my grandfather always had a "Couple." This was a husband-and-wife team of servants. The woman acted as cook and housekeeper while the man maintained the cars, did light gardening, and served at the dinner table. Most of the couples were African American (I think "Negro" was used at the time), but a few were Caucasian.

Dinner at my grandparents' house was a formal affair. My grandparents had their cocktails in the library at 6 p.m. Promptly at 6:30 the houseman would approach the library to announce, "Dinner is served," then we'd troupe down the hall and through the living room to the dining room and its large, formally-set table.

As soon as we were seated, my grandmother would step on the buzzer beneath her foot to signal the houseman to begin serving. During the meal, the buzzer would be stepped on multiple times, each time indicating that he was to appear to see what was needed.

I had dinner with my grandparents too many times to count, but I never got comfortable with this arrangement. I felt embarrassed and ashamed with the setup of "us" and "them," the served and the servers. I knew that it was important to my grandmother that I behave appropriately as one of "the served," but I had to pretend and put on a façade in order to do so. Fortunately, I figured out a way to find some comfort in all the formality.

I loved being in the kitchen and talking with "the help." It felt looser and more relaxed there than with my grandparents. We talked about interesting things, we laughed, and they let me help with the cooking. I'd go in there with the excuse of thanking them for dinner, but once there I just wanted to stay and stay. I liked them and felt liked by them. My favorite couple was Ike and Mary Louise, an African American couple who worked there for years when I was little. They were young, and I thought Mary Louise was beautiful. I got more warmth and interest from them than I ever did from my grandparents.

I was quite aware that my grandmother disapproved of my time in the kitchen, and she'd sometimes come to get me. At a young age, I was also clear that this had to do with race and class, although I didn't know those words. I just knew that being with her employees was wrong in her eyes, but not in mine.

Behavior is a powerful teacher, and children frequently learn unintended lessons from parents. JT writes of her parents as "civil rights activists who talked as though they believed in equality of the races. However, from the distinctions that happened in our home, I learned that it was not necessary to speak to people who worked for you as equals and that black people were not as important as white people." When a child notices that a parent's words and social actions are not in sync with that parent's behavior at home and there is no discussion about that difference, trust moves onto shaky ground and the child's sense of stability is threatened.

This is JT's story:

I grew up near Cincinnati in southern Ohio, right across the river from Kentucky and one of the most active chapters of Sons of the Confederacy. My parents were very active in liberal causes; one of them was working for civil rights. I was included in their participation. We wrote letters and marched in support. We watched television and were enthralled by the demonstrations and the integration of schools. We felt lifted up by the civil rights movement.

My parents were Oberlin College graduates, and my mom founded our local Unitarian church. They were cultured and wealthy and accepted their place in society. I never wanted for anything other than attention and understanding.

There were lively, often heated discussions with family members who were less progressive.

We'd hail Martin Luther King and Rosa Parks as heroes. They'd shout about Stokely Carmichael, Eldridge Cleaver, and Malcolm X. Usually, someone would huff away from the table. Although I hadn't yet heard the word "lesbian" (at that time, gayness was not on my radar), I knew, even then, that I was different and that I would be in trouble if my relatives knew that about me. When I think about being eleven years old then, the same age that my daughter is now,

I am glad that my spouse and I are parenting in the way that we do, that we're talking about things. Our daughter knows that we're both there for her, no matter what. At her age, I was so lonely.

When riots started to happen in Cincinnati, fear took hold. On the one hand, we sympathized with the rioters and understood the issues they were angry about. On the other hand, it was so scary and we were afraid that our lives would change. Even now, it is hard to hold the dichotomy of those two realities. I like my comfortable life and I want it to stay the same, even though I want the world to be better. I know that cannot happen unless we all make changes, unless those of us who have social and financial privilege are willing to give some of it up.

During that time, Catherine Henderson worked as my family's housekeeper and my babysitter. She was a kind, soft-spoken woman—a young African American, living with her husband and three sons in the poor black district of town. She always wore a uniform when she was at our house and my parents called her by her first name, just as they did all the black people who worked for us, even though they called my white babysitter "Mrs." They were civil rights activists who talked as though they believed in equality of the races. However, from the distinctions that happened in our home, I learned that it was not necessary to speak to people who worked for you as equals and that black people were not as important as white people.

There was always a lot of tension in my house. My parents' marriage was terrible for both of them. When they went through their divorce, Catherine was a safe harbor for me. I felt unconditionally loved by her, and being around her made me feel warm and safe.

I knew so little about Catherine's life. I wish that I had more specific information about her family. I think I resented them because she went home at night, rather than staying with me. They must have also resented us. I also think that she carried a huge load. It must have been very difficult for her to leave her own children and drive across town every day to work so hard doing everything for another family.

I don't remember ever talking to her about civil rights. I knew that with each civil rights victory, there were violent attacks on her side of town. Her son was beaten in one of them. I don't know if he was beaten by a policeman or by a white thug. I found out about the attack by accident.

Catherine died very young during heart surgery. We sent notes, but we didn't go to the funeral. It wasn't even considered. I feel so very sad when I think about how close we were in one way and how divided and separate we were in others.

Racism is a senseless and hurtful reality. As was true for Anne, Brenda, Bonnie, and JT, Natasha's close and loving relationship with the African American woman who cared for her during childhood was marked with confusion, pain, and significant separation.

Natasha writes:

When I was growing up in Philadelphia, my mother had a full-time job outside of the home, and when I was five years old, she separated from my father. They finally divorced when I was eight. My mom led a very busy life. To help with childcare and cooking, she hired Ruth, an African American woman. Ruth picked me up at the bus stop after school and I spent afternoons with her. On some days, those afternoons merged into evenings. I don't remember when she first came or how long she was with us, but I know she *was* part of the family and a trusted friend to my mother. I saw my dad on weekends and sometimes for dinner during the week, but most of the time I was with my mom and Ruth.

When I came home from school, Ruth was the person I told about my day. She was the one who first heard about my joy or pain. She was the person who took me to the store and gave me permission to play with friends. She was a loving presence at home day after day. I loved Ruth and knew she loved me.

And then—my memory is fuzzy here—she got very ill and couldn't come anymore. I wasn't told anything more about her illness. I missed her terribly. There was a big hole in my life, and I never saw her again. I asked my mom if I could visit her. The answer was no, with no real reason why. And when Ruth died, I couldn't go to the funeral—that's what my mother told me. My sense was that Ruth's life away from us was totally separate and so when she got ill, all my connection to her was lost.

I don't remember well my feelings then, but I guess it was sadness. Now, when I think about how the relationship ended, I feel angry. I am angry that I was kept from seeing Ruth. She was family to me, but no one really acknowledged that. In the formal separation of white and black, employer and "the help," in the adults' thinking, it was inappropriate for me to visit Ruth or to go to the funeral.

Having Ruth in my early life helped me feel safe and loved. I knew that there was another adult in my home who was there for me when my mom couldn't be. My mom had a lot of pain and anger around her divorce and Ruth provided me with a calm, loving presence during those times. My strong memory of Ruth caring for me and the love I felt for her has lived on.

The emotional distance that occurs when we first realize that family members whom we've loved and admired have thoughts and feelings opposite to our own can be painfully confusing and is often memorable.

Leslie shares her memories:

As a young girl hearing racist comments from my grandparents, I could really see how ugly racism is. I enjoyed being with my grandparents, but when they would make these comments, they would seem so ignorant and ugly. Suddenly, the people whom I cared for would repulse me.

I grew up in a white suburb of Los Angeles and I had very little contact with people of color. Still, I would confront my grandfather whenever he made racist remarks. I needed to prove them wrong. The African American people I knew were not like my grandparents said they were, so I knew they were wrong about other black people too.

When I see racism directed at another person when I'm not involved, it seems unfair. When I felt racism coming at my partner Army and me, as it did at a motel in Mariposa a few years ago, it knocked the wind out of me. Army is no longer living, but I still think about this. I felt so displaced by the racism, and when I saw that it didn't really faze Army, I really felt sad. She was so used to that kind of treatment that she took it in stride.

Being targeted by racism was new for me. It is very clear that Army received discrimination and outright hatred all of her life because her skin was brown. I have been receiving privileges all my life because my skin is white.

Diana also recalls a time during adolescence when her feelings about a loved relative were altered because of racism.

Diana writes:

One cold, rainy night in 1962, I left my after-school clerical job at a local hospital to wait for a bus in the dark. A young black orderly whom I sort of knew from the hospital and who was a little older than me offered me a ride home. With a little hesitation, I accepted his offer.

When my favorite aunt saw who brought me home, she warned me that "people might get the wrong impression and think that you go around with boys like that." Then, she said, my reputation would be ruined and no white boys would want to date me. I was confused and disappointed in my aunt. I loved her, but it hurt to have her turn a nice gesture into something bad. I even felt a little rebellious, but I was afraid that she might be right.

I assumed that her reaction would have been different if it had been a girl giving me a ride and I was sure of that if it had been a white fella.

Valerie, too, was a teenager when she learned of racist beliefs held by the father she loved and respected. Describing the dramatic shift in her feelings about him, she writes: "In my mind, my father became complicit with a terrible plague that blanketed my beloved country . . . and felt like tar."

This is Valerie's story:

Hough Avenue on Cleveland's east side was a hotbed of racial tension in July 1966. The area was populated with Appalachian immigrants and blacks displaced by urban renewal programs and tenement and rooming houses with absentee landlords. The 79er's bar at 79th and Hough Ave hung a sign saying "No Water for Niggers" and the bar manager and another man guarded the entrance with shotguns, and in so doing, fomented an already tense racial situation. On July 18, a black man entered the bar and bought a bottle of wine, but when he asked for a glass of water, he was denied. A group of fifty people protested this, as well as the manager's ejection of a black woman seeking a charity donation. When the Cleveland police arrived to diffuse the situation, tensions rose and rock throwing, looting, and vandalism eventually required police to call in the National Guard to manage the chaos. Over the next forty-eight hours, approximately 240 fires were started in a twenty-three-block area, four people were killed, thirty wounded, and three hundred arrested. This expression of frustration and rage echoed the 1964 race riots in New York City, Rochester, Jersey City, Paterson City, Chicago, and Philadelphia, and the Watts area of Los Angeles in August 1965. I was a naive sixteen year old with little direct experience with people who were racially or otherwise culturally different from me. I was, however, acutely aware of the unrest and outrage people were feeling around race and gender inequality.

On that hot July night I was horrified as I watched the black-and-white images on the old Philco of police beating people, black men and women, while surrounding blocks of buildings raged in flames. Tears streaked my face and sobs erupted from my chest as the reality of hatred, mistreatment, and poverty was expressed in the conflict. My father watched with me, and I was sure what was happening would make him mad too. What I didn't know was that his anger came from a different place.

He said, "What are you so upset about? Those niggers deserve what they are getting, they are destroying property and are so out of control the National Guard was called in!"

"But Daddy," I said, "why are they so mad, and why isn't anybody listening to them?"

"Whatever is the reason, they should do it different. Nobody handed ME a job, or built a low cost place for ME to live. They should fix up their places, get jobs, and stop living like animals. Maybe I'd have more sympathy for them then."

The conversation deteriorated into more of my tears and rage, and I fled to my room. I didn't want to live in a world that thought the way he did. I was grief-stricken that my beloved father had demonstrated such insensitivity; I had never heard him speak with such denigration about another person. At that time, I didn't know that his views were based on ignorance and bigotry, but I believed that he was wrong.

My family moved often to accommodate my father's upward mobility in his sales job and we had landed in Fairview Park, Ohio, a largely Caucasian and mostly Christian suburb on the west side of Cleveland. Throughout the first half of the twentieth century, my father worked with blacks, Hispanics, Italians, Greeks, and poor white migrant workers in the fruit packing plants, shipyards, and industrial laundries of the northwest. He perceived "minorities" (non-Caucasians and the poor) as lazy and stupid. I believe he was courteous and distant on the job and only spoke his racism at home. He was ambitious and probably competed with those minorities to prove himself a superior worker and management material. He never questioned the infrequent advancement or lower wages for people of color.

In my mind, my father became complicit with a terrible plague that blanketed my beloved country (which was supposedly rooted in a unique demand for equal rights for all) like a tar that stuck to too many reasoning people, justifying contempt, loss of basic rights, persecution, and psychological war. I felt helpless to change his thoughts or to stop the escalation of hatred and exclusion in America.

My awareness was magnified by media coverage of growing racial tension, civil disobedience, the Selma Movement, and Martin Luther King's 1968 assassination. By then, my heart was broken. I felt helpless and hopeless about the generational legacy of unquestioned stereotyping, profound separation and inequality, and evil maltreatment based on color and class. I was aggrieved that the leaders (John and Robert Kennedy and Martin Luther King) I'd had faith in to stop this terrible malignancy had all been assassinated.

I eventually forgave my father's unthinking words. I have also become doubly aware of the far-reaching impact of unacknowledged or passive racism.

I have been fortunate beyond words to have an African American friend who has been generous with her black literature, her family, and her personal racial struggles. She has always been diligent in her efforts to educate others about racism, as well as all other denigrating-isms. She led me to the National Coalition Building Institute where I trained to work with the wounds of exclusion. She helped me to incorporate the language of inclusion, non-judgment, and acceptance into my nearly forty years of psychotherapy practice. She has been there for me each time my sadness about painful memories surfaced and held my grief about the profound effect of racism in my life, alongside her own.

I still struggle with the heritage I received from generations of prejudice. It is so insidious that I can hardly recognize it in myself or in the myriad daily and ubiquitous messages about what constitutes "beautiful," "sexy," and "good." Class and race get intertwined into one debility and we allow degrading messages of "different is bad" to continue to be imbedded in the media and in the culture.

A biracial child whom I recently saw in my psychotherapy practice declared to me that the beautiful children at her school are the white kids with blond hair (like her mother), and so she couldn't possibly be beautiful. This came up around her "unmanageable" hair when I said that she was certainly beautiful, and she might just need some help with caring for her hair. She is growing up in a largely white culture where the few black kids at school "are all in special-ed." I watch her struggle to find identity in being tough or provocative as she uses swaggering television actors as models for her behavior. I see how she gets marginalized because of her hair texture, dark skin tone, and misdiagnosed learning problems. She has no personal contact with her father's family or any form of black culture. When I look at this child, I feel the weight of what she carries and I double my determination to be part of the solution. For her, for me, for us all.

2 Sameness

Prejudice is a shape shifter. It's very agile in taking forms that seem acceptable on the surface.

David Shipler, 1997

I knew . . . that in trying to shut the Negro race away from us, we have shut ourselves away from so many good, creative, honest, deeply human things in life . . . that the warped, distorted frame we have put around every Negro child from birth is around every white child also . . . that what cruelly shapes and cripples the personality of one is as cruelly shaping and crippling the personality of the other.

Lillian Smith, 1949

In this chapter, we highlight stories that address the cost of growing up immersed in whiteness, with little to no opportunity to question the racist ideology that is being taught or reinforced.

Fred's story addresses many of the different forms of social oppression: adultism, classism, male privilege, and racism. As a sensitive young male child, he was taught to be silent around the injustice that he saw, stifling his feelings with no hope of resolving his shame, pain, fear, and sadness. It has been his life work to unbury the hidden and repressed feelings and to give them air as well as mental and emotional space to heal. In so doing, he has reclaimed his humanity.

This is Fred's story:

This writing is not so much a statement as a process of identifying and attempting to name what is painful. I am a white Anglo Saxon male, born in Maine in 1941. My ancestors came to Massachusetts in the early 1600s, and both sides of my family evolved in New England. Having become part of an African American family forty-six years ago, I have had a more intimate view of the pain of racism than have most with my heritage. Part of marrying into an African American family is to be intimately exposed to the pain of racism on an ongoing basis and to marvel at all the victories so many African Americans have achieved in the face of death and unrelenting, life-threatening, humiliating, and vicious obstacles. I find it very challenging to separate racism from the adultism that installed it. During my childhood and adolescence, white supremacy (the tragic belief that whites are racially superior and should have dominance over other racial groups) was reinforced in all settings. We were taught to be obedient to adults and silent about our feelings, as well as to use addictive behaviors to ameliorate personal distress. It is clear to me that enforced separation from self and others is painful, regardless of the form that takes.

Learning from my parents to "do the right thing" and not be harmful to others assisted me in carrying enough self-consciousness to pause and see my own harmful behavior as well as that of others. However, it was not enough of a counterweight to the white supremacist education that was in the air we breathed or to the isolation from people of color in general. My head was full of glorified misinformation and partial truths about everyone, as well as an embarrassing amount of arrogance. It is hard to go right to what was painful and really remember the pain because we did not talk about what was painful or scary or uncomfortable. Where I have stories of fear and pain, there is also clear memory of a charged and deadly silence that is a reminder of all the things that affected us that we did not talk about. We were trained to be silent and to eventually model the ways in which our parents medicated. It was not just about race, but also about anything messy.

One of my two earliest memories of overwhelming emotional silence is of going on a country house call to the home of the one African American family in the small Maine mill town where my father was a physician. In the country, there were often long dirt driveways leading to isolated homes. It was dusk and our car lights were on. As we came within fifty yards of the small wooden house, a dark brown–skinned woman came running and screaming towards the car in the glare of the headlights. This was my first encounter with a person of color, and I knew her baby was very sick. Her fear was so powerful that it drowned the fear I was feeling. My father left me in the car as he went to help her and her baby. I felt overwhelmed, and I was stuck with addressing my feelings on my own. This would have been understandable if some concern for my experience had been forthcoming when my father returned to the car. He had helped the baby; I do not think the baby died. The unfamiliar woman looked calmer when she escorted my father out of her house. I needed some way to address my feelings and some guidance about how to integrate this new experience. We did not talk about it because my father did not offer an invitation or acknowledge that a very significant emotional experience might have happened for me. By that age, I had been well trained to not speak or ask for attention for my lingering state of overwhelm. We simply used the established pattern of dealing with feelings and emotionally messy situations in silence.

The other memory is of an experience at a summer camp for boys when I was ten years old. Ten to twelve boys in the same age group lived in cabins with older boys acting as counselors. The only boy of African American heritage attending the camp was in my cabin. He was nicknamed Pee Wee, a nickname he came with, I think. We had bunk beds and, sadly, Pee Wee wet his bed for the entire time that we were there. There was teasing. I can remember Pee Wee's frozen posture and everyone's discomfort as solutions failed and the mattresses hung out to dry did not dry and Pee Wee had no place to sleep. I offered to share my bunk with him because I thought it would not happen if someone else were there. I was wrong and, to my alarm, my bed got wet too. I can't remember how it all got resolved. I can only remember the uneasiness we were all expected to endure without discussion or comfort.

Both of these memories carry fear and shame and sadness that was never discussed or resolved. I was not able to bridge the unfamiliarity of these new-looking people because, in both cases, there was too much that was not said and could not be said without support. The enforced silence left me isolated with emotionally loaded first encounters that were not helped by the "white

supremacist" education I was getting. I learned to feel sympathy for these people and other African Americans, but not to have interactions that would lead
me into humanizing relationships. I would have to fight for those.

In going back through these early stories, I see the part they played in
isolating me from people of color by placing me in the "better than" position. A
wall of ignorance and arrogance was established throughout the social, familial,
and educational institutions in which I was indoctrinated.

This is what has been painful: the circumstantial and enforced isolation
that did not allow for the reality of anyone's humanity or for contact based on
that humanity. I was so full of misinformation and I had so much internalized
shame to overcome that it would be a journey for me to have a life in which
my connection with other humans would be based on shared humanity and
integrity. The effort to create a life inside of a white male social role was not just
about race, but also about accepting the package of privilege and isolation and
ignorance and arrogance.

Damage created by the legacy of slavery, Jim Crow laws, and institutionalized discrimination has been so great that there will continue to be some
degree of racial separation to the end of my life, regardless of my efforts to
close that gap. The hypervigilance that has been required for the survival of
African Americans continues to be experienced as necessary by many African
Americans even when it is not or when I like to think it is not. It is also painful
to see the continued presence of ignorance and arrogance in the white community. In a way, I think my whole life has been about climbing out of the pain
of white Christian isolation, ignorance, and arrogance to reclaim my given
connection to my own humanity as well as to that of others. What led me on
this path is a mystery. It is not that I want it to be mysterious; it is just that I
can give too many completely contradictory explanations that make sense. I
do know that I have consistently taken steps to build relationships across social and religious dividing lines and that I've always been rewarded for those
steps.

I always knew that something was wrong with the view of the world that I
was given during my childhood. The ability to reclaim that knowledge and to see
it as truth has been my reward for creating diverse relationships in my personal
and professional life. My current view of the world has far more integrity and

human pride than my early training left me with. My friendships and relationships with Jews, African Americans, Turks, Muslims, and Mexicans have been the biggest in terms of numbers, though the diversity of my relationships is greater than that. I eventually started hearing stories that moved me to broaden my ideas of the meaning of justice and love and truth and beauty, as well as to appreciate the depth of the damage of oppression and lies. I also learned that many injuries and generations of injuries take more than the one lifetime we know we have in order to heal. On the way, I learned that listening is more important than being right.

White supremacy creates a cocoon of fear and shame that is defended by isolation, misinformation, and ignorance. The power and value imbalance gets maintained, both aggressively and passively. This creates a painful separation from self and other that must be healed on both sides if it is ever to be transcended.

Many people who identify as white or have white skin privilege have strong memories of their first encounters with people of color. They stand out because of growing up in communities where people looked like each other and behaved in similar ways. When someone different showed up, it was noticeable and shed light on the surrounding sameness. Julianne's story highlights the loss she experienced in growing up in a segregated community, as well as her commitment to a more diverse community of friends today.

Julianne shares memories and insights:

When I was ten years old and in the fifth grade, I made friends with three siblings—the first African Americans I had ever met. Wynona, Thyme, and Ali were wonderful and amazing people. That's how I saw them. Not as black or white, but as great friends. I remember noticing that their mom was white. It didn't seem weird, just different. I remember asking them how come they had dark skin and their mom had white skin.

They told me that their dad was black and lived in New York. I accepted this without question, and we continued our friendship through high school and into adulthood. It was not until I was an adult that I felt a loss at not having been raised in a more ethnically diverse community. I felt deprived because I had been raised in a very white community, and I could count on one hand the number of black students I knew through my school experience. I recall meeting an African American man in college whom I was immediately drawn to and wanted to date. I believe I wanted to know this man better, not so much because of who he was as a person, but because he was a black person, and I cared deeply for the few black people I knew.

I recognize how sharing time with people of diverse ethnic backgrounds can enrich my life. I am grateful for the ethnic diversity of the people I share time with in my life today.

Life in a homogeneous community where honest conversations about racial oppression do not occur keeps white Americans ignorant of the social realities of people of color. When that is the case, coming into social consciousness is often painful. The following excerpt from "You Gotta Be Ready for Some Serious Truth to Be Spoken," Deb Busman's powerful essay about her experience of teaching an ethnically diverse group of college students that was first published in *Fire and Ink*, illustrates just how painful such an awakening can be.

Deb writes:

To teach creative writing and social action means you gotta be ready for the young blonde girl from a private high school in Sacramento's suburbs who rolls her Maybelline eyes the first day of class and says, "Is this going to be one of those courses where they try and ram that multicultural crap down your throat?" The same girl who, weeks later, sits weeping in class, heart and mind open, listening to shared stories of INS [Immigration and Naturalization Service] thugs and deported grandfathers and pesticide-poisoned baby brothers wheezing from asthma. Stories about cousins orphaned by police bombs dropped on fellow family MOVE members, seven- and nine-year-old brother and sister taken from their home, sitting in the Philadelphia police station, surrounded by cops watching the bombing live and in color on TV news, laughing, telling the children, "See those flames. See those tanks. That's your daddy inside there. That's your daddy we finally got right where he belongs." And the young, blonde, private high school student, who truly believed that California always belonged to the United States and that racism ended with the abolition of slavery, or at the very least after Martin Luther King Jr.'s "I Have A Dream" speech, turns her face to the class, Maybelline running down her cheeks, and says, "I'm so sorry. I didn't know. They never taught me about any of this. I'm so sorry. I just never knew." And her workshop buddy, Aisha, the self-described Pan Africanist revolutionary, takes the girl in her arms, rocks her softly. And Carlos, sitting in the back, can't help but shake his head, muttering: "Damn. And they got the nerve to tell me that my people are 'under-prepared' for college."

Those of us who grow up in whiteness are conditioned to believe in our "inherent superiority" and some of us attempt to teach our children these same lessons. Jeanne's story reminds us that it is possible for children to resist the systematic racist training of parents, thus staying true to their own hearts.

Jeanne writes:

I was born in Lincoln, Nebraska, in 1932 and raised there. At that time, Lincoln had a population of 1,800 that was primarily WASP (white Anglo-Saxon protestant) There was one synagogue and one Catholic church in the town. We belonged to a Presbyterian church and were called the "chosen frozen" because Presbyterians are so straight-laced.

Although my parents and I were the same color, we were not the same at heart! One of my earliest memories is of a time when my mother and I picked up my dad from work. While we waited for him to come out of the insurance company in which he was a life underwriter, I stood on the seat of our car and played with the steering wheel while my mother looked out of the window. I remember hearing her say, "Oh look at your dad! He walks just like a Jew." I didn't know what she meant, so she told me that he was walking with his feet pointing outward. She and my dad were always commenting on the appearance of others. When my dad would wash and polish the car, he'd say, "It shines like a nigger's heel." Whenever he shined our shoes, he'd make the same comment.

When I was nine years old, my maternal grandmother drove me to Omaha to hear Marian Anderson sing. She was very excited about this because she had heard that "the lady" had a really good voice. When Marian Anderson came out on the stage, she said, "I didn't know she was a Negro." She would never have taken me if she had known.

The music was so beautiful that I wept. My grandmother was so impressed with my weeping that she took me backstage to meet Ms. Anderson. Marian greeted me by saying "Hello. I love children!" and when I stood beside her, she covered my hand with her hand and I noticed that our hands were different colors. I was stunned in a beautiful way. It was like a jewel had touched me. I don't know any other way to describe the feeling.

It was also the first time that someone had spoken to me of love. Although my family was in church every Sunday, we never ever spoke of God or Jesus or love in our home. I never heard "I love you" from either of my parents. Most people say, "I love you, too" when someone says, "I love you," even when they don't really mean it. When I told my mother that I loved her, she didn't even do that.

There were two black students in my high school, a boy and a girl. Elbert Stark and I were very good friends. We would meet in the Teepee Room at the Cornhusker Hotel to talk and eat hamburgers. He was musically talented and very funny. My mother disapproved of my admiration for him. I never told my parents about our meetings and we were friends until he died. In 1951, three years after graduation, he committed suicide.

During my college days at the University of Nebraska, I volunteered at the Malone Community Center. It was on the "other side of the tracks." There were Dakota, Sioux, and African Americans there, although they were called Indians and Negroes. Indians were treated in awful ways, and no people of color came to downtown Lincoln during the day. I was very sad and very, very angry about the unfairness of the entire discriminatory life that we were living. I hated it and would weep openly when I heard about bad treatment. My mother would often respond to my tears by saying, "You are not of us." That also made me sad.

In 1961 and 1962, I was in California teaching second and third grade at Berkeley's Lincoln Elementary School, now called Martin Luther King Elementary School. Most of the pupils were African American. I had the same group of children for both years, and I really loved them. I learned so much from them. I wrote to my parents about the joy that I felt and, when they came to visit me, my father said that he didn't know why I liked being with those kids. He wanted to know how I would feel if a Negro raped my mother. He asked that question while we were in a restaurant. I walked out of the restaurant. When my mother came outside to get me, I cried and refused to go back in. She said that I didn't understand how frightened they were for me because I worked in the wrong part of town. I felt so imprisoned by my parents' attitudes. I wished that I had not invited them. My world was just opening up. Those children kindled my love for life and for being me.

At my invitation, year after year, Marian Anderson would come over from San Francisco during her annual concert at the Opera House so that I could take her to various schools to speak and sing. She was a profound figure for me, and we were friends throughout her life.

I continued to teach in Berkeley, and in 1968 I became the director of integration of the Berkeley schools. We had lots of meetings with parents and with the faculty and staff of the schools before we began to bus children. It all went off very smoothly.

Rosi offers us an understanding of how she came to be an ally to people of color. Her own experience with immigrating to the United States and being treated as "different" shaped her worldview and the choices she has made to break through the walls of sameness and be inclusive. Her story is also a reminder of how people who are afraid and do not feel good about themselves mistreat others.

This is Rosi's story:

Prior to World War II, my family emigrated from a small island off the coast of Finland to New York City: the New World, the city of dreams of safety, achievement, security, and opportunity. We left a cohesive community of some ten thousand people to come to a metropolis of more than eleven million. I was nearly eight years old, and not long after we arrived I was placed in a foster home so that my parents could work. My father became a laborer working as a dock builder on the piers of the city rivers, and he did not adjust to the diversity or size of New York easily. He sought instead the small organizations that contained people from his own country. My mother was a laundress in the homes of the wealthy and, for part of that time, she had a live-in job. She adored New York. "Adored" is not too strong a word, for she liked everything about the city: the diversity, the pace, the people, the sights and sounds and smells.

We were reunited as a family when I was ten. My mother made friends with some of the women with whom she worked, inviting them to our apartment for coffee and cakes. Most of them were white. My father's reception to the few who were not was to sit behind his newspaper and not acknowledge their presence, despite an introduction. My mother and I were very embarrassed, as our Scandinavian culture is a welcoming one. When I asked my father why he acted that way, he responded with racial putdowns. The matter became very personal when my biracial girlfriend was prohibited from coming to visit me.

I imagine that coming to a different country, not speaking the language, being in foster care, and not getting along with my parents had already contributed to my feeling that I was an "outsider"; there was no place for me in the world; I didn't belong. My father's behavior cemented empathy in my very being for those who were treated as if they didn't belong, the "foreigners" standing beside me who were human beings and yet different. When people are afraid of difference, they exclude.

When I went away to school, I allowed a person of color to use my room to study. Since I had apparently sullied the reputation of the more staid dormitory, I was forthwith moved to another.

Being young, a person experiences having little power. As an adult, I made a commitment to be an ally of "the different," "the outsider," because I, too, am that person. We need to stand together.

The following story takes us from a childhood filled with racial stereotypes and the accompanying fear of "the other" to parenting children who have had the benefit of growing up in a diverse community where there is an appreciation of differences. Where the story gets really painful is in the reality of a world where institutionalized racism is still very much alive, in spite of some of the progress we have made in developing more diverse neighborhoods. For Dana, a white male who grew up in an isolated white community, conditioned to be afraid of black and Latino youth, the internal drama of fear, anger, confusion, and sadness is yet to be resolved. This is how racism has impacted his life.

Dana writes:

In the summer of 1969, my transistor radio blasted out Top 40 hits all day, every day. "Patches," by Clarence Carter, "But It's Alright" by J. J. Jackson, "What Does It Take (To Win Your Love?)" by Junior Walker and the All Stars, and "Oh Happy Day" by the Edwin Hawkins Singers. I was a white boy in a small conservative town in rural Massachusetts and I LOVED black music! It moved my feet and my soul. And yet, although I was almost fourteen years old, I had never seen a black person except on television.

Reflecting on the impact that racism had on my childhood, I am left with a huge vacuum. My memories have only to do with racial stereotypes and imagined fear. To my knowledge, there was only one African American family in our town, and they were an elderly couple with no children. There were no Asian or Latino families and very few Jewish families. Although our high school symbol was a Nipmuc Indian (named after a local indigenous tribe), none of his descendants attended my school. Everyone was Caucasian, and most of us were either Catholic or Protestant. I had NO interactions with people of color of any sort until I entered college at the age of eighteen.

In hindsight, I realize that this made for a very bland racial experience. Since the eighteen years in question here are 1955–1973, there was plenty of political and cultural upheaval going on all around me. This was the era of the civil rights movement; Malcolm X; the riots in Watts, Detroit, and Newark; the Black Panthers; Rosa Parks; the Montgomery, Alabama, bus boycott; the

March on Washington; the Kent State killing; and the groundbreaking nonviolence work of Dr. Martin Luther King Jr.

One paradigm that I have pondered for years is questioning whether the fundamental roots of racism have to do with the simple concept of "otherness." This theory suggests that racial divisions begin with the simple notion that "YOU are not the same as ME! Your skin is a different color than mine. You talk in a different way than I do. You may eat different foods than I do." These differences, left unexamined, seem to lead to fear and distrust.

However, during my parenting years, I have watched young children play at the playground and I have seen little of that fear expressed. Little kids have curiosity perhaps, but not fear. They don't really seem to see color differences as meaningful. They have not yet been polluted with fear or racist ideas, attitudes, and opinions. They just want to play with each other and have fun!

Both of my sons went to a racially diverse elementary school in northern California. White kids were in the minority and my boys didn't seem to notice. At least, they never commented on it. It just seemed that racial diversity was woven into the day-to-day fabric of life for them. In one of his college entrance essays, my older son recently mentioned, "my circle of friends includes John, Juan, De'Angelo, Aamirah, and three different Ryan Fongs." It pleases me greatly that my sons have a racially diverse spectrum of friends. They seem to understand how that broadens their own lives and their perspective on the world. It makes me want to believe in the ways that the world seems to be changing.

It is at that moment of hopefulness that the world that I see as gritty and real always reappears.

On most workdays, I drive to a neighborhood in Oakland that is near a Bay Area Rapid Transit (BART) subway station. I park my car a few blocks away from the station, and, in the dark of evening after work, I make the fifteen-minute walk back to my car. Sometimes, if a group of young African American or Latino men are walking toward me, I think that maybe I ought to cross the street. I have a visceral reaction of fear as they approach. Are they going to harass me? Am I a target? First blood for a gang member? Do I just have an active imagination? I'm pissed and afraid and I bitterly resent having to fear for my safety. I wonder if I could defend myself, but I know that I'm no match for a knife or a gun. I think about my friend who got the shit kicked out of him in this same BART parking lot about a year ago. He has a physical disability. Two predatory creeps saw that he had a limp and they preyed on his infirmity. He gave them his wallet and they beat him and kicked him in the head anyway. He had done nothing to them. He was just walking to his car, minding his own business. This memory makes ME want to hurt somebody.

Around and around the fear, the violence, and the reprisals go. We have all endured centuries of hating and mistrusting each other. We have all felt afraid and in danger. When I finally arrive safely at my car, I let down my guard. Sitting quietly for a moment, my mind circles around, once again, to the hundreds of years that black people have felt constantly afraid while living in this country and walking on these same streets. I think about the ignorant, vicious white racists who dragged James Byrd Jr. for three miles behind their car to a gruesome death in Texas a few years ago. So many people have experienced fear, judgment, violence, and death just because their skin was not white. I think of Rosa Parks, Medgar Evers, George Jackson, and Rodney King. I'm aware all over again of how the lack of day-to-day exposure to people of color in my own childhood continues to mess with my head and my heart in my fifties. I'm also painfully aware of how it makes me feel angry, emotionally conflicted, and confused. And tomorrow night when I walk through these streets to my car in the dark, I'm sure that I will go through this whole elaborate dance with myself all over again.

As Caroline reflects on the ways in which her relationships with people of color have changed during her lifetime, she shares thoughts and feelings about growing up in de facto segregation.

This is Caroline's story:

I am most struck by the feeling of loss when I think about the impact of racism on my life. While I am deeply grateful for the choices I have made in my life that have brought me to a place where I am connected to people of color, my upbringing was racially isolated. The first African American woman I met was Dathrene, the woman who cleaned our house. We loved each other. I can still remember her warmth. But she did not live in our neighborhood, nor did any other black people. She worked for us, as did the gardener from Mexico. As a small child, I did not question this. I thought this was the way it was, because in my small corner of the world this was what I saw and experienced all around me. I do remember thinking that it did not make a lot of sense to me, but since there was never any discussion in my family or in my community about the social separation or why it existed, my small child mind accepted that this set-up was the natural order of things. I was an adult before I learned about "red lining," the deliberate creation of segregated housing communities that benefited whites and marginalized people of color.

So when I speak of loss, I speak of loss that involves both my heart and my head. The loss from the heart, the realization that my world kept me separated from people of color, is deeply painful. The loss that involves my head, all the information and learning that I did not get when young, produces feelings of shame and remorse. As my adult life has allowed for much interaction and relationships with peoples from many different races and cultures, I often reflect on how much I was deprived of as a child. I consider my upbringing to be one of privilege, but it is a limited definition of privilege when you examine what I did not have the opportunity to experience. I still feel as if I am in a catch-up course on life.

3 Guilt

Sometimes there was brutality; sometimes there wasn't. But the whole system turned on violence.

Edward Ball, 1998

The anger of the oppressed man is a sign of health, not pathology. It says: "I am condemning you for doing wrong to me."

Alexander Thomas, MD, 1972

Americans who grow up in all-white communities generally receive a great deal of direct and indirect racist conditioning. That conditioning is made up of damaging misinformation that dehumanizes people of color and lingers in the minds of white Americans long after their first interracial experiences with peers. Generally the misinformation creates a strong element of fear that deters self-examination and adds to isolation and the perpetuation of "white guilt."

"White guilt" is a consequence of being part of a dominant and historically oppressive group of people. Sometimes it adds to self-hatred that gets projected outward onto people of color. Sometimes it creates a kind of paralysis, stilling any movement toward cross-racial friendship and social and political consciousness. Sometimes it causes white people to identify with people of color so strongly that they reject their own whiteness and, in so doing, reject themselves. All of this contributes to confusion, misunderstandings, and the lack of meaningful conversation about racism and racial issues. Frequently, this guilt is passed on to children.

Any time that I get totally wrapped up in my own feelings of guilt and fear, I am unable to move forward as an ally because I am so busy thinking about myself that I am unable to think about others. If I carry "white guilt" and behave in hurtful ways that come out of my racist conditioning, and someone points this out to me, chances are that I will not be able to take responsibility for my behavior. I may become defensive. Rather than looking at what I have said or done, I may blame the targeted person(s) with accusations of being "overreactive," "too sensitive," or of "taking what I said in the wrong way."

In order to fully address racism and racial issues, white Americans need to be able to move past old fears and guilt. Stories in this chapter address the lingering guilt experienced by these writers as they struggle to unlearn racist conditioning.

Liz's story is powerful in its demonstration of how oppression works: one small child, feeling powerless over a bigger child, uses the power she does have to inflict pain. Decades later, Liz still struggles with her feelings about using racism to deliberately attack her schoolmate, demonstrating, once again, that we cannot inflict pain on others without hurting ourselves in the process.

Liz writes:

When I was in second grade, I attended a school where, strangely enough, running and skipping were forbidden on the playground. One day I began to skip unconsciously, skipping being my preferred mode of transportation at the time. I heard a shriek and turned to see a fifth grade stranger in a frilly white dress and pristine knee socks crying out for a teacher to discipline me. I was suddenly aware of both my transgression and my grubbiness. With shame rising in my face and seeing doom approach in the purposeful stride of a teacher, I struck back in the only way I knew. I called my accuser a name. I remember searching for the right name to level the awesome power wielded by this perfectly coifed, perfectly starched, taller, stronger, and obviously more disciplined girl. Like David before me, I found just the right projectile to hurl. "Nigger," I said. I didn't even know what it meant. I just knew that she was black and you weren't supposed to say "nigger" to a black girl because it was mean. But "mean" was exactly the point in this situation, and I felt desperate. Like David's stone, my epithet hit with deadly force. My opponent's face crumpled, her awesome power washed away by weeping gushes of tears. The teacher turned from disciplining me to comforting my victim, and I wandered away forgotten, horrified and guilty at the pain I had caused. I think it was the fact that she dissolved into tears instead of flying into a rage that opened me to a sudden empathy. Decades later I still awaken in the middle of the night, heart pounding, wondering what deep wounds I might have caused this girl and wishing I could apologize. If there were an Internet site for reconciliation, I would post this story there in the hope that this woman, or someone like her, might see the suffering and transformation I incurred as a result of my racist act. This was the last racist epithet I ever uttered. Even the thought of this episode makes me feel sick.

From Leon, we hear the remorse and lingering guilt over his adult behavior as he acknowledges a time when another man's compassionate behavior shone a light on what he, Leon, was unable to do.

This is Leon's story:

I have always had a few black friends, Japanese friends, Korean friends, and so forth. I have been a man of compassionate response some of the time. At other times, I cowered from action and watched with guilt.

I almost ran over a very drunk Alaskan Native man who was passed out and sleeping on the highway on a dark drizzly night. I swerved and braked, pulled my car over, got out, pulled him off the highway, and began yelling at him, asking if he knew I almost ran him over. Another man stopped, came up to us, knelt down to this man, held his head, and asked his name and where he was from.

Lynne's story speaks important truth about the cost of growing up in segregated white communities: the confusion, the silence, the lack of accurate information about or real relationships with people of color, the false belief of being "one of the good white people," the inability to "get" racism or understand that it has anything to do with you, and the guilt that accompanies sensing that something is not right but being unable to figure out what. Fortunately for Lynne, her life has held valuable experiences that have allowed her to make changes in both her thinking and her actions. Her struggle to move past guilt is a life-long journey.

Lynne writes:

I was born in 1950 and grew up in a small town in Indiana—a mid-century, mid-American, Wonder Bread (literally as well as figuratively) kind of childhood. As a child and young teenager, to the extent I knew or thought about racism, I didn't think it touched my life. It was about places where there was segregation and the fight to end it. It had nothing to do with my small town, where everyone went to the same junior high and high school and believed in "liberty and justice for all," as we pledged every morning in school. So it's only with a retrospective adult eye that I can see how racism played a part in my life from my very early years.

Looking back from first memories through mid-life, I can sum up the effect of racism on my life in three phrases: confusion mixed with fear; guilt and self-blame; separation and disconnect.

I remember being at my grandparents' farm when I was four or five years old and being told I couldn't play outside because "the Mexicans" were out in the field at harvest time, and they might kidnap me. I remember looking out of the window at the farm workers. I don't know what my thoughts were at that moment, but I do remember that when I was a bit older, I thought back to that time and wondered why they'd want to kidnap me.

Later in my childhood, I heard my dad talking about an older man who worked at a restaurant we frequented, saying how he was "a hard worker, even though he's colored." "Hard worker" was the ultimate compliment in my middle-class Midwestern family, and I knew my dad seemed to like and joke around with the guy. I wasn't sure why being "colored" made a difference. Also at about that same age, I remember my parents locking their doors in the car and telling me to lock mine in the backseat as we drove through certain areas of downtown Indianapolis on our rare excursions there. I don't remember an explanation, but they only said it when we were in "the colored" neighborhoods. At home, we never locked our car or our house. These vivid memories and my confusion are mixed with the vague sense of danger that accompanied the experiences. I don't have any memories of my parents offering any explanations or of my asking any questions. They fell in the category of unspoken rules learned during childhood, things I somehow felt I should understand but didn't.

When I was thirteen, my family spent a year in a suburb of Miami, Florida. I went to ninth grade in a middle school that was in its first year of being desegregated. There, all of my friends or their parents were transplanted northerners. One day in the locker room after gym class, a white girl with whom we were acquainted but who was not our friend spit in the direction of one of the black girls and refused to take a shower because black girls had used the shower. I remember feeling shocked and embarrassed. None of us said anything at the time. There was just an embarrassed silence. Later, one of my more knowledgeable friends said, "That white girl is a cracker and that's why she acts like that." However, when I moved back to Indiana for the rest of high school, I realized that there were some white kids at my school who had similar attitudes. They came from families that had moved up from the South to work in our town's Firestone factory. By then I knew to classify them as "rednecks" and to separate the "bad" white people, when it came to issues of race. During my late high school and college years, I had some growing awareness of civil rights and events beyond my small Indiana town upbringing. However, most of them seemed to be very distant.

One memory from my senior year in high school is of the day after Martin Luther King's assassination. Kevin was the only black kid in the art club, and he usually had a smile on his face. I can't say we were friends, but a core of us "arty" types would hang out in the art classroom together in order to "cut" sports assemblies. Since that group included Kevin, it seemed as though we had a bond. One day when I walked into art class, I saw Kevin slumped in his seat. He sat with his head in his hands during the whole class. I felt like I should say something but was afraid to say something wrong, so didn't say anything. I don't think we ever spoke to each other again. A vague sense of guilt is attached to that memory. It is as though I betrayed him, but I didn't know what to do about it. Maybe that one memory is so vivid because it is that feeling of guilt and confusion about feeling guilt that would be intertwined with my relationship to racism for years to come.

During my early years of college, guilt and self-blame came full force. Again, a vivid memory comes through the fog of confusion. My first semester freshman "forum" class was "Race in America." I had done the prerequisite reading for the class over the summer, so I wasn't as ignorant and naive as I might otherwise have been. I remember feeling a vague unease on the first day as I tried not to look at the few black students in the class. As the course progressed, we studied and discussed in detail the history of slavery and the genocide of Native Americans. For the first time in my rather insulated life, I heard the directly voiced anger at the system from the black students. I felt a sense first of embarrassment and then of guilt growing from inside me for being white. Again, it was mixed with confusion. Exactly what was I guilty of? What should I do? I was in a fog.

There was one black student in my dorm section during sophomore year and sometimes we'd hang out together at the dorm, drinking beer and playing cards. One day, while crossing campus, I ran into her while she was with a group of other black students. I said "Hi," and she looked away, pretending she didn't know me. What I took from it was that I was an embarrassment to her in the eyes of her friends. More to the point, I felt that I deserved to be. Being white made me a bad person in the eyes of people of color and also in my own eyes. I was "getting" that I wasn't "innocent" as a white person, just because I wasn't a "redneck" or "cracker." However, I had neither the context in which to place that awareness nor the emotional or psychological tools to do anything with that knowledge other than to get mired down in guilt about it.

I tried everything that I could think of. I tutored Native American kids at an inner-city center in Minneapolis, and I volunteered at refugee camps when I was in Lebanon on junior year abroad. I guess those actions could be summed up as typical "white liberal" things to do. But although my intellectual understanding of racism, colonialism, and their many threads grew, on the emotional level that undercurrent of guilt and self-blame remained. During my time in Beirut, however, I did a lot of discussing, theorizing, and just hanging out with fellow students from all sorts of backgrounds. There were students from all over the Arab world, Asia, and North Africa; black and white American students; European students; and ex-patriots from Europe and the United States. That time was invaluable to my growing sense of racial consciousness.

When I left the activist atmosphere of college life, I gradually drifted away from taking any relevant actions, and I also drifted away from friendships and other meaningful contact with people of color. That was not a conscious decision, but it seemed to be an easy path, for as I went about my job and life, I was "naturally" just around other white people. Looking back, it also put those feelings of guilt and self-blame way in the background.

Sometimes I think that without the Beirut experience of having connections with such a diverse group of people, I would have just kept drifting along that easy path. However, I did know better than to think that having just white people in my life was "natural." I don't remember what brought it up for me, but I do clearly remember walking along the recreation trail in Pacific Grove, California, and feeling in my gut my disconnection from the wider world. It was a feeling of loss and separation from so much of humanity. That was a moment that let me know I had to do something to find a way to bring that diversity of connection that I knew was possible into my life again.

In the years since then, I've expanded my life out enough to be part of the diversity. I've learned about the dynamics of racism as it plays out in our lives, not just as political theory. I've done a lot of psychological work on my white "patterns." Sometimes I still feel confused and guilty. At times, I still feel that old sense of disconnection, and I can get a little crazy wondering what people of color think of me. The good news for me is that now I know that this is the result of the particular ways that racism affected my thinking and experience of the world as a white person. I know that it's not "reality" in the deep sense of what is real about me and about the whole diverse world of other people.

Patricia offers us a painful example of the personal consequences of her father's racism and her own. Growing up in racial isolation left her unable to effectively cope with a difficult conversation with an African American woman. That important moment jarred her awake and ultimately changed the course of her life. Although it took many years, she developed the consciousness to better understand her experience and her unexamined and unfounded fears, and she made a decision to continue to move forward with broadening her life.

This is Patricia's story:

I grew up in a small, rural, all-white Oregon town. The one exception was a Nigerian exchange student who was full of fun and whom all the students liked. Occasionally, my father spoke angrily against black people. I remember looking at him askance, thinking that he was being weird and making no sense whatsoever.

I had never lived in a big city before my husband and I moved with our small daughter to Long Beach, California. In 1968 I was attending night school after working all day to put my husband through Long Beach State College. The August 1965 Watts Riots had happened three years earlier, before a late-night incident on the Long Beach City College campus shocked me into a new reality, albeit it one I did not understand. A classroom interchange with an African American female student brought up racial fears and guilt and caused me to quit school and led me into decades of inauthentic relationships with African Americans.

That night in my speech class, the teacher divided us into groups of six, with instructions for each group to choose a topic on which to give our first speech. As we went around the circle of the group I was assigned to, each of us gave an idea of what we thought would make a good topic. We then discussed each idea and expressed our opinions about its suitability. I've always been friendly and outgoing, and I gave my opinions freely that evening, sometimes agreeing, sometimes not.

All went well as we discussed various ideas until I voiced my opinion of a young black woman's idea. When I disagreed with what she said, she jumped up and screamed, "We black people have been suppressed by you white peo-ple for more than four hundred years, and I won't take it from you any longer." The outburst frightened me out of my wits and I was dumbfounded and could not speak.

Later, on break, as we stood around in groups, I noticed that this same young woman was standing quite close by within a group of tall black men. She was speaking animatedly to them. She appeared to be looking and gesturing my way. After class, I had to walk a long way to my car. It was in a dark parking lot and I was alone. I remember being frightened and thinking she may have asked those men to hurt me—or worse! I quit school and never went back there.

My father's outbursts and television coverage of the four-day Watts Riots had instilled a great fear in me of black violence. I knew that black people had plenty to be angry about. My fears have been unwarranted; no African Ameri-can has ever harmed me. The young woman's words made me feel guilty about the centuries of bad treatment of blacks by whites, so I began to treat them differently. I was artificially super-friendly for fear they would think that I, too, was prejudiced. I suppose that I wanted to ameliorate some of the sadness I presumed they carried.

I came to see my behavior and my thinking as prejudice of a different sort, inauthentic and unhelpful and probably unkindly transparent as well. I am angry about the racism that was instilled in me and very sad about the suffering that has been caused to all peoples.

I finally realized my dream of a college education twenty-five years later when I enrolled in the Monterey Peninsula College. Later I transferred to the University of California at Santa Cruz, where I received my bachelor of arts in philosophy.

I'm learning to treat all people with the same kindness and friendliness I wish for myself.

Joe's story is a poignant reminder of how much work we still have to do to dismantle the racist system that surrounds all of us. Many years later, Joe still struggles with guilt about his inability to change racial injustice done to his friend and fellow basketball player Wilt Chamberlain. Although Joe admits to feeling "not big enough" to change the institutional racism that privileged him at the expense of Wilt, his story also demonstrates the strength and power of personal relationships. He and Wilt were friends for life.

Joe writes:

It was midwinter 1954–1955 and a thin, seventeen-year-old Wilt Chamberlain, a high school senior, was making news and stirring talk the sports world over. He'd scored ninety points in one basketball game for Philadelphia's Overbrook High, and coaches and other experts were speculating about where he would go to college. *Life* magazine ran a photo centerfold showing him and half a dozen or so other prep players, all of them around seven feet tall, cradling basketballs above their heads as a ball rested in the bottom of the net. All the young players except Wilt were white. They looked gawky, anemic, or bulky, like shot putters, compared to him. Wilt's body looked sculpted, gleaming, athletic, strong, and quick. We knew he was going to be a mighty star.

I was a tall basketball player that winter, too—only six feet nine—and I wondered how I'd do playing against him. In June, I was, I thought, to find out. I'd been picked to play in the nation's only high school all-star game a few weeks after graduating, and I worked hard to get ready to practice with Wilt during the week before the game in Murray, Kentucky. He was a graduating senior that June, too.

Wilt didn't show up. At a meeting in the Murray State College gym that advertised both the North and South's teams for the press and public, every player on the rosters was white. Word spread fast that the good burghers of Murray chose to let the South be the South and forgo bringing the first Negro player to the all-star event.

I came from Princeton, Illinois, a town of 5,800 souls founded by progressive New Englanders and the site of an Underground Railroad station set up by an abolitionist, Owen Lovejoy, about whose fame we were puffed with community pride. I was sixteen years old and green. I was disappointed to see for myself that this was how the world was run where racists were in charge. I felt ashamed. I felt that the rhapsodizing I heard almost daily about the promise of America during those prosperous Eisenhower fifties was false. I felt guilty and helpless, emasculated by the rules of segregation, angry that my basketball brother, a big center, a young man dreaming of playing at a college or university like Kansas or Northwestern, was handcuffed, chained, symbolically still under the lash along with his people. Eighteen months later I slid into a folding chair alongside a long, institutional table in the Kansas University cafeteria. Next to me sat Wilt Chamberlain, looking like he was wearing football shoulder pads. He stuck his hand out toward me and mine got lost inside it.

We were facing a dozen reporters in a press conference about the next night's game. It featured his Kansas team against my Northwestern team in what would be Wilt's college basketball debut.

He chatted with me before we turned to the press. I apologized to him. "I stood in your place in Murray," I said, telling him that he, not I, should have played center for the North. He told me to forget it and said that I had earned the honor of having been selected after the game as the nation's prep All-American center. "You earned it, man," he said.

I felt worse, as if I'd let Owen Lovejoy and my hometown community down, as if I had a duty that I was unable to carry out by permitting racism to flourish in connection with a high school game. I felt worse than I did after the game we played the next night, in which Wilt scored fifty-two against me. Fifty-two points, a testament to his ability that still stands as the most ever scored by an individual in a KU game. I didn't feel guilty at all about what he achieved, or about the fact that we lost and lost decisively. I felt guilty about racism, and yet our friendship that began at that press conference would flourish.

More than twenty years later he gave one of my children the jersey he wore in his college basketball debut. "We're friends," he told me. More than thirty years later I was the only opposing player he invited to ceremonies celebrating the retirement of his uniform number by KU in October 1998, less than a year before he died. "I'm always glad to see you," he laughed when we greeted each other. "I scored fifty-two against you."

I could do little to stop the assault on America's principles by bigots except stay true to mine, to remain a friend to Wilt Chamberlain, and to honor his memory. I feel guilty to this day.

He was bigger than I am. He endured insult and indignity, as did his fellow African Americans. I try to rise to the occasion when I witness ugly violations of our principles of justice and brotherhood. I always try to defend them, and too often am left feeling guilty that, like that night at KU, I'm not big enough to join decent people in triumph over racism.

Among the many challenges facing white people as they begin to understand racist conditioning are the unconscious ways in which they act out feelings of superiority or entitlement. Molly was ultimately able to hear how her behavior affected an African American colleague. Although she feels guilt as she considers her behavior and regrets what she did, Molly is also willing to admit that what she did, even unknowingly, was racist.

Molly shares her experience:

At twenty-eight, I was working as a caregiver in the school-age parent nursery at a high school in Ann Arbor. Six of us had charge of about fifteen children between the ages of six weeks and two years while their parents—mostly unmarried mothers—were in class. My coworkers were all African American women my age or older. All of them had grown up in Detroit's poverty-stricken black neighborhoods.

After lunch, when the babies were settled in for naps, the staff took breaks by turns. One day Tasha, who was on the shift with me, responded to a knock at the door, and then turned to tell me that her friend had arrived, having driven from Detroit so the two of them could go to lunch together. Tasha was getting her hat and coat when I told her she should wait until our coworker, due back from break in a few minutes, arrived. I reminded her that we were supposed to have two staff in the nursery at all times. Tasha finished getting ready and left.

At our next staff meeting, Tasha was furious. From her point of view, I was a newcomer and an outsider and had no business telling her what the rules were. If I'd been there more than a few months, I would have known that the culture of the agency allowed for some discretion, especially in these circumstances. She experienced my directive to her as racist, grounded in my sense of entitlement as a white person. I was white, she was black, and, therefore, I was the boss.

For days afterward, I was in turmoil. At the time, I thought it was Tasha's anger alone that shook me. After a while, I realized that the deeper and more disturbing dimension of the experience was the accuracy of Tasha's perception of me. I had acted from a sense of entitlement based on the color of my skin and the circumstances of my upbringing and a sense that what she had brought to the interchange was "less than," was inferior. Now, I wish I could take it back.

Bob's story offers deep insight into the roots and consequences of virulent racism. Motivated to understand the racist culture he was born into and to rid himself of the shame and guilt created by growing up in that culture, Bob has become an icon of the civil rights movement and continues to speak out against racial injustice. He has come close to physical death many times because of that commitment. Yet, in our first conversation, when he spoke of the impact of racism on whites, he spoke of the "murder of the soul."

This is Bob's story:

When I was asked to write about how race discrimination has damaged white people, my mind was forced to shift gears. We usually confine our thinking to how racism has harmed those it is directed against, and I had never thought about the ways in which I was harmed. In reflecting on my assignment, however, I am realizing that racial hatred's persistent, deep stain on our present and past has hurt us all.

I grew up in south Alabama, the cradle of the American Bible Belt, where children were to be seen, not heard. We lived in our own little world, separate from adults for the most part, except for the occasional housekeeper or babysitter. Talk of race, religion, philosophy or politics was out of earshot of little people because, Grandma Hardy said, "Little pitchers have big ears." Such secrecy was scary, causing me to feel vulnerable and insecure. The notion that there were things on this earth that even Mom and Dad had no power over made me afraid. Infidelity, violence, scandals, and such were discussed, if at all, in hushed voices—not openly like today.

Our own family scandal was Daddy's "nervous breakdown." I don't remember how my brothers reacted to Dad's malady, but insecurity and dread caused my intestines to telescope, according to the local doctor. That psychosomatic condition caused me intense abdominal pain. Southern families have always been famous for the eccentric bachelor uncle or maiden aunt locked in the attic wearing only Confederate gray or antebellum gowns. Mental disorder was scandalous and something to be ashamed of. Southern writers have mined this trove for decades.

The South, big on appearances due to the prevalence of mental illness, reveals the other side of Fanon's study of mental disorder. Frantz Fanon studied and wrote about imperialism and resulting mental disorders among oppressed people, but no corresponding study has looked at the mental illnesses of the oppressor.

Dad's participation and membership in the Ku Klux Klan (KKK) was, without doubt, a primary cause of his breakdown. You can't be a minister of the gospel and practice racial hatred without paying a significant psychological price. Although the Klan connection was never mentioned, Dad's dilemma, like the American one, was preaching one thing about race while doing another. Having half the population lording over the other half, taking the best of everything while leaving the rest to make do on scraps, was bad enough. But my father had also figured out that holding black people down was impoverishing a majority of white people. He began preaching that if you were a poor, working-class white person in the South holding the black man down in the ditch, you should realize that you are down in the ditch with him. A rich man, Dad said, walked down the center of the road laughing at both men in the ditch—the black one and the white one.

Wealthy people, remembering the "patty rollers" of slavery times, were content to let "white trash" do the dirty work. Before the Emancipation Proclamation was signed, common whites, owning no slaves, were often paid by slaveholders to patrol the roads looking for runaway slaves. They were called patty rollers. Ne'er-do-well white folk gained a false pride by having more social status than the "niggers." And, they thought, "One never knows, I might just own me some slaves someday."

This is much like today when many poor and working-class white Southern males of a certain age support the right-wing policies of Republicans dictating low taxes for the richest Americans. "You never know," say these dreamers, "I could be rich someday myself, and I would not like to be taxed."

As little boys, my brothers and I had no idea of racism and its possible connection with our father's sickness. We just knew something was wrong with Daddy, and we wanted him to get better so he could play with us again. I felt abandoned and not worth very much, what with Mom busy teaching and being "the minister's wife" while Daddy was absent a lot. We didn't understand that Dad was undergoing a crisis of conscience.

Dad's family and surroundings had determined his identity, wrapped up to an unusual degree in "the race question." Raised in Birmingham, a raw, bustling, industrial cauldron, he grew up in a relatively young city unleavened by the noblesse oblige paternalism sometimes found in older Southern metropolises. Young James Abraham Zellner was not exposed to even the tiny liberalizing influences I found during my high school days in Mobile. New Orleans on the Gulf Coast and cities of the Atlantic seaboard, like Charleston and Savannah, were much more cosmopolitan and relatively sophisticated. Granddaddy Zellner was a telegrapher and later a dispatcher on the GM&O Railroad, a hot bed of Klan activity. He taught his three sons and two daughters to be white supremacists. As the oldest son, my father pleased his father by becoming, after initiation into the secret brotherhood, a Klan organizer, or Kleagle, with responsibility for recruiting new members.

As a child, then, I was injured by the system of apartheid in America. My injury, however, was not as apparent or as immediate as the damage being done to Mom and Dad. Dad, ambitious to do well in the ministry, was torn between advancement professionally on the one hand and his emerging conviction that racial oppression and discrimination were both immoral and un-Christian.

Before I started school, we lived in Newton, Alabama, which was near Dothan, the economic hub of southeast Alabama and parts of the Florida

Panhandle. I have no conscious memory of race ever being discussed or even mentioned, but in later life I have had flashes of memory of virulent racism from that time. The memories consist of horrible screams of pain and loud whacks like a whip hitting a telephone pole. When asked about these things Mother said I could be recalling scout initiations. Dad was involved, as were we boys, in scouting.

I remember names, events, and places, whispered in hushed conversations. Apparently, adults were unaware that little ears perked up when voices dropped to a whisper. Usually people spoke of Franklin Delano Roosevelt openly and proudly but sometimes in hushed voices: "He's trying to stop lynching . . ." or "Neal . . . Claude . . . Neal . . ."

In college, I studied sociology, psychology, and history, and I did graduate work in sociology at Brandeis University. During all those years, I grappled with the emotional toll that others and I paid for growing up in a Southern "paradise" that seemed peaceful on its surface, but that was anything but peaceful and serene. Later, working on a doctorate of history at Tulane University, a discipline that demands a clear-eyed look at one's specialty (in my case Southern history and specifically civil rights history), I found it impossible to ignore my racist past and that of my beloved Deep South.

A cowl of shame descended over me when I learned it takes a village—no, an entire region—to raise and maintain a system of economic exploitation based on race and the circumstances of one's birth. Mom and Dad, big on shame and its uses, often chastised us with "Aren't you ashamed of yourself?" delivered in the proper tones of disappointment. This was a feared consequence of even the most minor infraction.

The shame I felt as a white Southerner, however, that my people had systematically injured and beaten down a whole other people was exponentially worse and of greater magnitude than small shames, like the time I was caught playing "doctor" with Linda Barnhill, a parishioner's daughter.

My feelings of shame changed to an aching guilt that I had benefited from the misery of others. As a young teenager, I had tried to imagine how black boys my age could deal with their rage toward white bullies. My only fear in dealing with bullies was that they would beat me up unless I was successful in beating them. Young black men, feeling their manhood, were told by their elders not to fight back because it might cost them their lives. White men might kill them for being uppity, or they might disappear into the prison archipelago stretching across the South. Prison labor was such that businesses and plantations bought and sold convicts just like in the old days of slavery.

While researching and writing *The Wrong Side of Murder Creek: A White Southerner in the Freedom Movement*, a memoir of my experiences as an adult in the civil rights movement, I could not avoid asking why so few white Southerners took part in the front lines of the struggle that came to be known as the Second American Civil War. Why did white Southerners leave the heavy lifting to our black brothers and sisters and their Northern allies? Why were the overwhelming majority of Germans "good Germans" during the Holocaust? One day I tried to think of a white Southern slaveholder who, at the height of his or her power, wealth, and political influence, freed his slaves to become an active abolitionist. I confess I could not find a single one.

Answering my own question, I reasoned that during slavery, whites across the nation, especially the South, maintained that institution through force, violence, and terror. To enslave a fellow human being is an act of war against that person. In order to war against a person or a people, it becomes necessary to learn to hate that person, "those people."

In order to own a human, as opposed to say, a mule, the owner or slaveholder must deny the humanity of that man, woman, or child. So, growing up in south Alabama among a people who had, for centuries, practiced treating people like objects or mules, I was expected to do likewise. In order to accomplish this degree of dehumanization, the ruling race suffers a shriveling of its own soul and spirit. Over time, farm children, trying to get over their tenderheartedness when killing chickens, rabbits, pigs, and other livestock, manage to harden their hearts. In the same way, many Southerners get over their innate dislike of mistreating others. They teach themselves and their children, "Blacks aren't the same as you and I, and so it is okay to mistreat them."

Eventually, in an effort to gain understanding of my memory flashes of childhood, I looked up racial incidents that occurred in southeast Alabama when I was little. Maybe, I thought, something happened before I was born that people were still talking about. Perhaps there was something so horrible that it still lives in the unconscious of the people of Alabama and northwest Florida.

I came across the following, which could explain my earliest memories of the problems of race and the South. I will condense and paraphrase to remove some of the horror surrounding the death of a twenty-three year old black man in south Alabama, just before I was born. Walter White, the courageous anti-lynching NAACP investigator, uncovered this horrific story while launching a national campaign against lynching.

On October 19, 1934, Claude Neal, a twenty-three-year-old peanut farmer, was arrested for the murder of Lola Cannidy, twenty. After confessing under torture, Neal was moved to a jailhouse twenty miles away, supposedly for safekeeping; the lynching spirit in the region was high. But in the middle of the night of October 26 he was removed from the jail by lynch mobs, driven about two hundred miles, and dumped on the road in front of the Cannidy home. Neal was tortured for ten or twelve hours.

Railroad companies in several Southern states laid on special trains, transporting thousands to the scene of the "lynching party" in southeast Alabama. The owners, happy to turn a profit, may have felt like ticket sellers at the Roman Coliseum, where Christians were fed to lions, but that feeling is not recorded in the NAACP records. Needless to say, merchants in and near my hometown must have had a field day supplying thousands of mob members with rope, food, and drink.

Neal's body was tied to a rope on the rear of an automobile and dragged over the highway to the Cannidy home. Here, a mob estimated to number somewhere between 3,000 and 7,000 people from eleven Southern states was excitedly awaiting his arrival. When the car dragging Neal's body came to the Cannidy home, a man who was riding the rear bumper cut the rope.

A woman came out of the Cannidy house and drove a butcher knife into his heart. Then the crowd came by, kicking him; some drove their cars over him.

Little children who lived in the neighborhood waited with sharpened sticks for the return of Neal's body and, when it rolled in the dust on the road that awful night, these little children drove their weapons deep into the flesh of the dead man.

Later, Claude Neal's body was hung high in the town square, casting a long shadow over the seething crowd. In addition to being a possible explanation for my earliest memories of the problems of race and the South, the grisly case of Claude Neal illustrates the emotional and spiritual damage that racism and its practices have inflicted upon my family and to me.

Imagine an entire region of people who mistreated black people, a mild and profoundly understated way of describing the terrible institution of slavery, from 1617 to 1865, a period of more than two hundred years. Now, think of the same people re-enslaving black people under Jim Crow and the sharecropper and prisoners-for-purchase systems for the hundred years leading up to 1965.

If you can imagine growing up in such a region, you will have some understanding of what I experienced. That was the region of my childhood and adolescence and those were the people—friends, fellow church members, family, and acquaintances—I grew up around. They were people so steeped in racism and self-hatred that nothing was as it seemed to be.

Would not such people have shriveled hearts? Small hearts don't have room for the milk of human kindness. It is difficult for me to believe that these are the people I grew up with and looked up to. Has human kindness dried up in Southern white people?

Is this why the South today constitutes a lowland where acidic puddles of racist poison stagnate, especially among the older population? Only 10 percent of white people who voted in Alabama pulled the lever for our first black president, Barack Obama. White Southerners still call him "the foreigner," thus rejecting the legitimacy of a black president.

How different is it today from the time that Claude Neal was the forty-fifth lynching since FDR entered the White House on March 4, 1933?

Separation during Childhood and Adolescence

One of the best-known songs from a Broadway musical is Rodgers and Hammerstein's hit from *South Pacific*, "You've Got to Be Carefully Taught." As the lyrics say, racist conditioning of children is sometimes intentional and direct. It can also be instilled indirectly and unintentionally. Since young children have no emotional boundaries (i.e., no way to protect themselves from the emotions of others), strong negative feelings such as hatred and fear will be absorbed from their caregivers. Punishing and humiliating children while keeping them from expressing anger at the perpetrators of such mistreatment will encourage them to lash out at others whom they see as vulnerable and powerless. Over-control that stifles their natural curiosity will not only discourage the development of intellectual interests and artistic endeavors, it will also support resentment of difference. However, if the evil of hate and the sickness of irrational fear are not instilled carefully enough and early enough, and if there are other powerful influences in the child's life which contradict those teachings, these debilitating lessons may not be permanent ones.

In the stories that follow, white adults look back at their childhoods and share how they were affected as children by their parents' ignorance and racism. In every story, the issue of separation is present. For some, friendships with children of color were not allowed; for others, relationships with parents suffered dramatic change. Even the most hopeful story addresses the issue of emotional isolation and physical separation from people who are different. Growing up in totally white environments damages the hearts and minds of children even when their awareness of racism does not come through witnessing or being actively and intentionally taught racist beliefs and actions.

Some children are so deeply conditioned by their parents' attitudes that they adopt that same perspective. What might have begun as deference for their parents' beliefs can slowly become absorbed as the child's own thought process. For children who are able to think differently and who continue to stand up for their own beliefs, living with parents who overtly espouse racist thoughts may become intolerable. Although Diane grew up in a hateful and hurtful home environment, she was able to find support for developing a different way of feeling and living.

Diane shares her story:

I grew up in Chula Vista, California. In the summer of 1963, I had graduated with an Associate of Arts degree from Stephens College in Columbia, Missouri, and was working and living at home until the fall, when I was to attend San Jose State. I remember a conversation at the dinner table in which my father was espousing his racist beliefs (My father was not only racist, but also sexist, anti-Semitic, homophobic, alcoholic, brilliant, narcissistic, and physically, emotionally, and sexually abusive to his children. He reminded me of a Nazi. I was terrified of him but also idealistic and sometimes rebellious.). I said that I didn't think that other racial groups (African Americans or Hispanics) were inferior to us. He said, "When you have to support yourself, you will see what I say (i.e. that other racial groups are inferior) is true." I thought about that. It didn't make sense to me. I said, "I want to support myself." He said, "You can't until you graduate from college." My sisters and I were to go to college to meet and marry rich husbands. The authority in his voice let me know the conversation could go no further. I was quiet.

I decided to take out the money I had saved from teaching swimming lessons all summer and exchange my ticket to San Jose for one to Washington, D.C., where my friend lived. I knew that I had to support myself *now*, and I was afraid. I couldn't tell my parents where I was going because I feared they would stop me.

A few weeks later my boyfriend took me to the airport where I boarded a plane to Washington Dulles International Airport. My friend's family took me in and said I should call my parents and let them know where I was. My younger sister, who was still living at home, was traumatized by my father's rage during that phone call. I was disowned, no longer part of the family.

I received a scholarship to Capitol City School of Nursing at D.C. General Hospital and spent a year in Washington. I became a Bahá'í because their sociological beliefs about the equality of all races and women were in alignment with mine. I was also the president of the freshman class. However, it was still a very lonely, difficult year. I isolated myself and took long walks alone. I went home the following year, but I never reconciled with my father. He died of a brain tumor two years later when I was pursuing my first year of teaching, supporting myself!

In thinking now about myself as a nineteen-year-old girl, I realize that the blatant racist opinions my father expressed that evening were a gift in that they woke me up. I grew up with his cruelty, but it wasn't until that dinner table conversation that I became conscious of the flaws in his thinking and that he was a sick man. I had not developed the confidence to understand that I had a right to differing opinions. I loved my father. I wanted and needed acceptance and respect from my parents, regardless of the differences in our social and political viewpoints. They were incapable of that, and I made sense of what happened by believing they didn't love me. I did not believe that they could treat me the way they did if they loved me. My mother complained about Dad's drinking and his DUIs, but she never admitted he was an alcoholic. Although she was an educated woman, she didn't believe she could support herself and four children in the manner she wished. She wanted to maintain her social and financial status. She loved my father and had suffered from the divorce of her parents as a child. I don't think she could face the truth.

Fortunately, I'd had a childhood experience of being neighbors with Mrs. Casey. She was a thoughtful, kind, and compassionate woman who was the mother of the Catholic family living across the street from us. She created a safe home, and my younger sister and I were allowed to play there. I remember her delivering clothes to an African American family with many children after their mother died and their father had to raise them alone. She expressed acceptance of all races, and she had a deep influence on me.

By the time I was nineteen, I had also spent two years at Stephens, a very good women's college. I had been exposed to people from all over the country. I had studied sociology, ethics, humanities, and current events. I gained support for my respect of all groups, and my best friend was a civil rights activist. That summer, she was taking a bus to Washington, D.C., to march with Martin Luther King Jr. While she was fighting for equality, my father was espousing beliefs about inequality. I was furious with my father and knew deep down that I could not let him control me any longer.

I feel grateful for my decision to leave home and realize it was necessary for me to develop as an autonomous human being. I feel sad that it was impossible for me to connect with my father through mutual understanding.

Fortunately for Susan M., her parents waited too late to instill racial fear. Even though they interrupted her early interracial friendship, the joy of that relationship formed a basis for her ability to embrace racial difference in adulthood. Like Diane, Susan M. had an adolescent experience with parental racism that deeply affected her. It provided an awakening to the connection between mistreatment based on racial difference and that based on social class.

This is Susan M.'s story:

I recall that it was springtime in the first grade. A big bunch of us kids used to invent games to play at recess. We had begun playing a cowboys and Indians game. Actually it usually became two rival gangs of cowboys. We'd gather, four or five boys and girls mixed together in a group, and go galloping, hands slapping hands and then legs to make that clippity-clop sound, chasing after each other across the play yard. Eventually, one gang or the other would get ambushed with "bang, bang, bang" from the rival group, resulting in hands clutched to chest followed by a dramatic dying fall. Then, they'd pop back up to play again.

The gangs would form as soon as we ran onto the playground. Usually, I was part of a gang that included my classmate Andy Sanchez. I liked playing with him because he was quick, inventive, and played fair. More often than not, Andy and I would emerge from the schoolyard door at a gallop, collecting gang members on the run as we headed for our first rendezvous.

I usually had a friend or two over during the afternoon, or I'd hook up with kids in the neighborhood. A variety of boys and girls came to play at my house after school. However, the first time that I invited Andy, he was the only friend there. We galloped around my backyard for a while, and then I showed him how to play a game I'd invented in the driveway of my house. It involved hitting a ping-pong ball with a paddle against the garage door. Andy picked up the complicated rules quickly, and we had a good time. After a while, he left to go home.

My father arrived home somewhat later, and just before dinner my parents called me into the kitchen. My mother said that I shouldn't ask Andy to come over to play after school again because it wasn't a good idea. I was definitely not to repeat the invitation. My parents had never told me such a thing before. Though it was never stated, I knew it had something to do with his Mexican-sounding name and that we were playing out front where the neighbors could see. I was indignant and thought my parents were making a big deal out of something that was no deal at all. But I never questioned them and never asked Andy over to play again. In fact, I avoided him, though I tried not to make it obvious, because I was afraid he'd ask to come to my house again, and I didn't know what I would say.

The cowboy game soon gave way to a vigorous dodgeball game, and then it was summer vacation. The next year, Andy was no longer at my school.

The school I attended was very white and located in a part of town where the houses were large and the families wealthy. My parents were not wealthy. Our house had been one of the first built in the area. I was five years old when my father designed it and a contractor friend helped build it. My parents were always proud of the fact that they had managed to get into the neighborhood before the prices soared. The important reality for me was that my friends always seemed to have more stuff than I ever had and that they got to go on fabulous vacations.

I had two best friends, Carol and Patsy, who often invited me to spend long, lazy days at the country club while their mothers played golf. We met in kindergarten and spent endless hours together over the years, on up through the eighth grade. Carol could run the fastest, I played the piano, and Patsy always managed to become the teacher's pet. We grew up from little kids to budding teens, sharing it all.

Then, in the summer before the ninth grade, I didn't see Carol or Patsy for several weeks because they were away with their families on long vacations. Finally, shortly before school was to begin, we got together. Carol and Patsy were talking in an unusually secretive manner about some activity they were doing. Apparently, they didn't want me to know about it. I finally asked what they were whispering about, and they said they were taking a charm and modeling class. Secretly surprised that they would be doing this without any mention of it to me, I said, gosh, that sounded interesting, and I wanted to know more about it. They exchanged knowing glances, blushed with some embarrassment, and brushed off my inquiry by stating that the class was very expensive. In that instant, although nothing else was ever said, I knew that their parents had told them that I was not to participate in this activity. This was a class to groom them as young ladies of their social class, and I was not a member of it. During that school year, they began to avoid me while trying not to make it obvious. Eventually, Carol was sent off to an expensive girls' boarding school and Patsy left with her family to live in Europe, but by then our friendship had already faded away.

Parents pass on their prejudices and children are the victims. Andy Sanchez and I clasped hands across time.

Childhoods spent in communities that lack racial diversity create social handicaps. Like Diane and Susan M., Carolee grew up with people who looked like her and her family. It was not until she was a teenager that she became aware of being hurt by her father's racism or of the loss that was created by living with racial sameness.

Carolee writes:

I grew up in the Midwest in the 1950s and 1960s in a community of thirty to forty thousand Norwegians, Germans, and people from other countries in Western Europe.

It was the early sixties, and I was in the ninth or tenth grade. Small towns would send their basketball teams to play against teams in other nearby towns. On one Friday evening, my friends and I went to the game. Lacking interest in the sport, we spent our time walking to the concession stand and wandering the halls looking for people we knew or didn't know. When a boy smiled at one of us we would say, "Oh, he likes you!" and we'd giggle and go back to our seats. Then we'd get up and walk by him again. This would go on for much of the game.

One night, a boy from the other team, who had also come to watch the game, smiled at me. My friends got excited saying "He likes you." He was standing with a friend, our eyes met and he smiled. I thought he was kind of cute. We smiled at each other and then looked away until the game was over. When my friends and I walked out after the game, I saw him again and he was close enough to talk to. We exchanged names, phone numbers and small talk. He asked if I would go to a movie with him. We parted and I figured he would never call, especially because he was from a town about a hundred miles away.

He called, telling me that he didn't drive yet and asking me to meet him at the theatre. I was very excited and said yes. But when I asked my dad for permission to go and told him that the boy was from Sisseton, South Dakota, he immediately became angry. He shouted, "Only Indians live there. It is on a reservation. Indians are all drunks; they never work; they are lazy and live off the government. You can't go out with an Indian."

I explained that he had red hair and freckles and I didn't think he was an Indian. Needless to say, I was very confused and very sad. He seemed like a nice person when we talked on the phone. I went to my bedroom and cried because I was so disappointed. I was extremely angry with my Dad and wondered how he could say those horrible things about someone he had never seen. I don't know how I got permission to go. Perhaps I lied. Perhaps my mother just let me go.

When I met him at the theatre, I was frightened and sad because I kept thinking about what my Dad had said. I did not have a good time. I didn't like him. I know now it was what my Dad said that influenced my feelings. I never saw him again.

As I look back, I still remember my feelings of anger and sadness. We could have at least been friends.

Despite growing up with an alcoholic father who raged when he drank, physically abused his wife and children, and preached racial hatred, Jerry was able to get support from people who helped him develop a life that includes positive self-esteem, loving family relationships, and interracial friendship.

Jerry writes:

My dad used the N-word every time he referred to black people. When the neighborhood kids were hanging around together, he wouldn't let me play with the black kids. I was really confused. It didn't make any sense to me. I didn't understand why there was any difference.

My father drank a lot and was physically abusive, so there were a lot more things to worry about with my dad than his racism.

I was lucky because my mom had a different attitude. When Mom started having black friends, he gave her all kinds of shit for it—he even unfairly accused her of having affairs with them.

Also, when I was thirteen or fourteen, people who came into my life helped me see things differently. I started to work at Head Start, a federal school readiness program for young children, and to think for myself, and I came to see how wrong my father was.

Leon's short story underscores how subtle the teaching of racism can be, so subtle that the confusion of being separated as a result of racism still lingers in memory.

Leon writes:

I was thirteen, and my parents bragged about their tolerance for people of all colors. After all, "my father was a captain at Fort Bragg and all the (colored) soldiers loved him." So I brought Sheila Espy home to our cottage as my first date . . . she was black . . . real black and beautiful. She was also fun and innocent like me. Her family played music across the lake that we could hear in the evenings and they danced as a family. So here I was, having Sheila come to dinner and my parents welcomed her and fed us. Sheila and I went off after dinner to the lake where we swam and played like thirteen year olds. It was my only date with Sheila. I don't know why.

Sometimes, caregivers of children who grow up in communities that have no members of racially targeted groups make efforts to instill attitudes that include acceptance of racial difference and that protect their children from the ravages of hatred and fear.

Maria shares an early memory:

I grew up in a rural community with children of people of Japanese ancestry recently released from World War II internment camps and with children and grandchildren of Holocaust survivors. However, there were no African Americans in my community.

I remember being three and a half years old, groggy from anesthetic after eye surgery at Children's Hospital in San Francisco. The first person I saw was a stranger, a large black lady leaning over to pick me up. I screamed. The next thing I recall is sitting on the lap of a blue-eyed blond nurse, drinking milk from a carton through a straw.

When I recovered enough to return to our rural home outside Petaluma, my progressive Aunt Ruth brought me a little black rubber baby doll. It actually looked just like my pink one, except with a tan. Even at that tender age, I understood that I had hurt the dark-skinned lady's feelings and that my aunt didn't want me to be afraid of black people. I played with both dolls until I outgrew them.

<hr>

Linda's heartfelt writing offers us vignettes from her seventy years of living. From reading her stories, we gain an understanding of the ways in which she has been impacted by racism as well as the ways she has resisted its teachings. Her stories also reveal her need to be seen as a good person and the deep shame she carries about her racist conditioning.

Linda writes:

"Ring around the Rosie," we chanted in the churchyard, holding hands and dancing in a circle. "Pocket full of posies. Last one down is . . ." I cannot bring myself to write it; I can scarcely believe the words ever came out of the innocent mouths of three- and four-year-old white children, myself included. We fell cheerfully to the ground. At first I misunderstood the words to be "Last one down is a nibble baby," but I suppose my Sunday school teacher "corrected" me. Ironically, it was at church (in Denver, early 1940s) that I learned the N-word, with no one guiding my moral compass or teaching me to question the mindless lyrics of a children's ditty. It was one of the subtle ways in which little white children were gently led into a racist and segregated society. [Editors' Note: The traditional version of the verse ends, "Ashes, ashes, we all fall down."]

At that age, I assumed "N-baby" was an acceptable name for little black children, just as I assumed "pickaninny" was also fine, since it came from adult mouths. But by age five or six, I knew those were not good names. I also heard unfriendly stereotypes from adult mouths: "Negroes were lazy and smelly, drove Cadillacs, dressed up super-fancy on Sundays, and were poor." I observed that Negroes lived in separate parts of town called "colored town," where poverty was, indeed, obvious even to a child.

There was a lot of poverty in the 1940s, regardless of skin color. Hoboes would knock on our door asking to do painting or yard work. Mother would give them work, then serve them soup and a sandwich at our breakfast-nook table.

The only color I saw in those men was the color of poverty and despair as it penetrated every skin type. I came to realize that the N-word was used—not by my parents, thank God—with derision and a lack of respect. When my mother had a party and I heard women calling the Brazil nuts "N-toes" (not "nibble-toes" as I hoped I was hearing), I was shocked, offended, and pained by their lack of sensitivity.

During my childhood, I rode with my mother to deliver and pick up our ironing at the home of our "ironing lady," a lovely, dignified woman named Mrs. Greentree. Later, when I was old enough and tall enough, I did our ironing myself. We ironed everything back then: blouses, skirts, dresses, pants, pillowcases, sheets, tablecloths, napkins, petticoats, and my father's heavily starched blue work shirts. It was steamy, tiring, back-pinching work, and yet my weekly labors were just a fraction of what Mrs. Greentree did daily. Inside her house, a hot, almost scorched smell permeated the air, and clotheslines were strung around the periphery of the living room, full of ironed clothes for white folks. While she and Mother chatted, Mrs. Greentree's strong, big-boned hands never set down that iron, never stopped pressing out those white folks' wrinkles.

I loved going with my mother to Mrs. Greentree's house. The homes in her tree-lined neighborhood were large and made of quarried stone, probably originally built for wealthy white people and later inhabited by Negro families because of "white flight." Mrs. Greentree had several kids; her family needed the space. When Mother and I went there, I always wanted desperately to play outside with Mrs. Greentree's children and the other neighborhood kids while Mother and Mrs. Greentree visited, but nobody ever suggested it. I felt an invisible barrier that made no sense to me. I was sad and disappointed to never get to play with those children. They seemed so happy in their games.

When my parents suddenly felt it was time to "upgrade" to a new house, just five blocks away from our first one, they said it was to have a larger home and be a little closer to the high school. It was 1954 and there were whisperings that Negroes were about to move into our neighborhood. Although the new house really was bigger and a somewhat shorter walking distance to East Denver High, I was fourteen and indignant that my parents might in any way be a party to "white flight" fears.

Many embarrassing elements of racism wove in and out of my 1940s–1950s childhood. I am uncomfortable as I remember them. Born the year before the United States entered World War II, I had no awareness that America had herded its Japanese-American citizens into relocation camps. I had no idea until well after the war was ended that the term "Jap" was pejorative or that black Americans weren't allowed to fight alongside white Americans. My grandfather, a pharmacist, owned a drug store in a small farming community in southeast Colorado, where I heard the word "Mexican" used disdainfully by white farmers chatting around his pot-bellied stove. Occasionally my mother would negotiate a bargain and say she had "jewed somebody down." Appalled, I chided her into dropping the demeaning term from her vocabulary.

Even as a youth, I understood the immense power of our words, for good or for evil. Today I shudder at the mindless, often violent rhetoric of people who are irrationally angry with our first black president, Barack Obama. The depth of racism in our country troubles me deeply; I am often reminded of the song from South Pacific, about having to carefully teach children hatred of people who are different from them. How, I ask myself, HOW can we teach parents to teach a different message, to stop perpetuating hatred? How can we cleanse their hearts of the racism they were so carefully taught at a tender age, so they can keep from poisoning their children's hearts with it?

To my eternal shame, a small cartoon-like picture in watercolor and India ink hung in our house during my early childhood, drawn by a former neighbor. Because he had presented it to my parents framed and ready for hanging, I suppose they felt an obligation to hang it somewhere in the house. It resided in my sister's basement bedroom for a few years before being relegated to the attic. There was some praise for the artistic skill of the painting, but never any discussion of its content. It depicted a black man seated on a log, wearing red-and-white checkered trousers, a green shirt, red suspenders, and large shoes; his hands and face were India-ink black, and he held in his hands an enormous slice of watermelon. The caption, in artistically formed letters, read: "Yassuh, ah sho' loves watermelon!" It is humiliating to acknowledge what that piece of art represented: the insensitive and racist conditioning of my childhood.

Sometime during my teen years, some of my girlfriends cajoled me to join Job's Daughters, an offshoot of the Freemasons (My grandfather was a Mason and my father a reluctant and inactive one, which qualified me to be a Job's Daughter). I knew nothing about Job's Daughters or about the Masons because both were secret organizations. It never occurred to me to question whether they were open to people of all races and persuasions. I assumed that anybody could join. But there were no girls of any color except white in the group and I don't think there were any Jews either. My major enticement for joining was that I'd get to wear a pretty dress for the initiation ceremony. It was my first formal. Soft and pink. Innocent. Naive.

We daughters of Job met in the majestic, stone-cold, marble-columned Masonic Temple, where each of our meetings began and ended with pomp and circumstance: singing, a processional and recessional, some knocking on doors and scriptural quotes, and the officers sitting at a monstrously big dais. I became an officer, the librarian, whose duties included researching and writing essays (usually about history or morality), which I read at each meeting. We officers wore—oh dear—white satin robes belted with white satin cords. The content of the meetings was semi-religious, never racist, yet there we were, a group of white girls sitting around being secretive and smug. I lost interest within months and dropped out. I like to think that if I had known for one second that it was an organization restricted to Caucasian teenage girls, I would have burned and chaffed at the injustice and resigned immediately.

Deborah shares the story of her deepening understanding of the costs of racism to white people as she recalls childhood memories.

Deborah writes:

At a diversity training in 2001, ten months into the process of working on the Diversity @ OSU website, I became acutely aware of the sorrow I felt about racism when I recalled an early childhood memory of my friendship with two African American boys named David and Darryl.

It was the mid 1970s and we were living in Mercerville, New Jersey, a predominantly white suburb of Trenton. I met David and Darryl at the bus stop when I was ten and instantly liked them both.

After school, we played "Kill the Man with the Ball" and wrestled almost daily in our front yards. We were like three puppies. David was grounded quite often, so Darryl and I tended to mostly play together. When we weren't wrestling, we played "Rock 'em Sock 'em Robots" in my garage. I had a crush on both boys, but since I saw Darryl most often, my affection was directed toward him.

One day, less than a year after I'd first become friends with David and Darryl, Darryl and I were outside in my front yard wrestling on the grass when my mom came home from work. She got out of her car, said hello to us, and then went in the house. Later that night after Darryl had gone home, my mom and dad invited me to sit down with them at the kitchen table, the place where we tended to have serious talks. They asked me not to wrestle with Darryl anymore, and I didn't question or challenge their request. After that evening at the kitchen table, David and Darryl and I stopped playing together.

When I recalled this memory in 2001 at the diversity training, I felt a great deal of sorrow. I had absolutely no recollection of any interaction with David and Darryl following the conversation with my parents at the kitchen table. When I tried to remember how we stopped playing together, there was nothing but a feeling of emptiness. I couldn't remember any conversations with them, playing "Rock 'em Sock 'em Robots," or walking to the bus stop. There was numbness. When I was able to get underneath the emptiness and numbness, I knew that my loss of friendship with David and Darryl marked the beginning of the distancing and loss of relationship and intimacy with people of color and with myself. I felt grief.

Following the diversity training, I decided to call my mom and ask her about her memory of what had happened to my friendship with David and Darryl. I called her, shared with her my memory and the grief I felt, and then asked, "Mom, why did you ask Darryl and me not to wrestle anymore?" My mom responded, "I knew you'd ask me about that at some point and I've been afraid that you'd think it was because of race." There was a pause and then she continued, "I was scared that you and Darryl would cross the line of play and innocence and that you would end up in a situation where you were unsafe." There was another pause and then my mom said, "When I was in eighth grade I played with some [white] boys the way you and Darryl played together. One day, we crossed that line of play and I wasn't safe anymore. They pinned me down, bounced a basketball off my head and tried to take my pants off. I was afraid that could happen to you. I was afraid that you would think this was about race, but I couldn't let you wrestle with boys given what had happened to me. I needed to protect you." I then asked, "Do you remember what happened to my friendship with Darryl or do you remember what happened to their family?" My mom gently replied, "I don't remember, Deb."

After I finished talking with my mom, I felt sadness because I had just learned that she had experienced a violation of her body and a loss of safety and trust with some white boys at a young age. I also felt dissonance and guilt, because, despite what my mom said, I did think that, in addition to gender, race and racism was at work regarding my parents' request that I stop wrestling with David and Darryl. I did not want to impose my point of view on my mom by insisting that race had something to do with why she asked me not to wrestle with David and Darryl anymore. She believed that her reason was for the maintenance of my physical safety as a girl verging on adolescence with two boys, and I respected her belief. At the same time, deep in me I knew that race and racism mattered. Given an enduring history of stereotypes of African American men as dangerous, rapacious, and predators of white women, a stereotype that still haunts the psyches of white people today (including my own), I believed that this would also penetrate the psyches of my parents who were born in the mid- to late-1940s and who were raising a daughter through the late 1960s and 70s. I also wondered about the protection and safety of David and Darryl. What protection existed for them from the irrationality, fear, dehumanization, and violence of stereotypes born from white supremacy?

I also reflected on how racism was used to reinforce sexism in relationships between white men and women. In the late nineteenth century, white men, in order to assert their power and control of white women, claimed that white women needed protection from black men, often assumed to be sexual predators. In part, the subjugation of white women was reinforced through creating and perpetuating fear of African American men.

This reflection led me to the memory of another event in my adolescence with some white boys whom my parents assumed were safe. Shortly after the loss of my friendship with David and Darryl, I began hanging out at my friend

Delila's house after school. Her parents worked, so we had the house to ourselves. Her brother, Ralph, was several years older and he was also there. Often, Ralph's friend Tim would come over too.

One afternoon, Ralph and Tim decided to instigate wrestling and chase Delila and me around the house. Neither Delila nor I wanted to wrestle, but Ralph and Tim persisted despite our yelling at them to leave us alone. Delila bore the brunt of the unwanted wrestling. As the wrestling escalated, Ralph and Tim pinned her and tried to pull off her shirt. She was shrieking and terrified. I screamed, "Stop" and then grabbed her brother Ralph by the hair and pulled him off of her. Tim stopped what he was doing and both boys got up and left the house. Delila and I were assumed to be "safe" with these two white boys. One was Delila's brother, and yet we were far from safe.

When I sit with the memory of wrestling with Darryl, a black boy, I feel warmth and sweetness. When I sit with the memory of wrestling with Ralph and Tim, two white boys, I feel fear. When I reflect on the historical and contemporary use of racial prejudice and stereotypes directed toward black boys and men to reinforce the dominance of white boys and men in order to control the lives of girls and women, both white and black, I feel I might vomit a brick that contains the costs of racism and its relationship with sexism and other forms of oppression. Loss of intimacy, authenticity, life-affirming relationships, human dignity, and love are such huge costs for us all to pay.

Three years after I first recalled the sorrow I felt about the loss of relationship I felt with David and Darryl and people of color due to racism, my family (my biological mother and father, their spouses, and my partner's mother) got into a conversation about race in our kitchen while my partner and I prepared Thanksgiving dinner. They were sharing stories of witnessing racial prejudice. On the one hand, I am relieved that my family was talking about witnessing racial prejudice rather than making racially prejudiced comments (which has occurred at previous family gatherings). On the other hand, I am concerned that we white people who resonate with the idea of racial diversity and justice tell stories of witnessing racial prejudice to reinforce the notion of ourselves as "good" white people. Thus, we see ourselves as opposed to the few "bad" white people and we distance ourselves—emotionally, intellectually, and spiritually—from learning how we have internalized racism and of its costs to our humanity.

I had been listening while preparing dinner and decided to take a break and stand next to my father, who was also quietly listening to the stories. I placed my hand on his shoulder as I stood next to him. I had been there for a few minutes when he turned to me in the midst of the conversation and said, "Deb, remember when you used to wrestle with Darryl in the front yard? I remember pulling into the driveway after work and seeing you two wrestling. I felt uncomfortable because Darryl was black." In that moment, I felt an upwelling of gratitude for my father's honesty and vulnerability in examining how he struggled with his racism. He validated my thinking that, in addition to gender and sexism, race and racism mattered in the memory of my lost friendship with David and Darryl. In that moment with my dad, we shared a return of intimacy and authenticity in our relationship, and I felt less alone.

Through participation in a native philosophies class and by witnessing the impact of colonization on the people of the Republic of the Marshall Islands during a time when I lived there, space opened for my unacknowledged grief and despair about racism to finally surface in my consciousness. I often questioned the authenticity of what I felt because so few white people in my life seemed to understand the depth of my feelings.

"The Soul of White Folks," written by W. E. B. Dubois in 1920, discusses the emotional and spiritual devastation that white people experience when they begin to acknowledge their participation in a system of dominance—"an inhuman set of practices and beliefs over five centuries of European hegemony."[*] It was only after reading that essay that I began to trust the authenticity of what I felt.

Deborah continues to explore her own history and previous inability to feel or talk about issues of race as she examines the impact of growing up in sameness and the childhood separation that brought her so much grief.

---

[*] Mab Segrest, "The Souls of White Folks," in *The Making and Unmaking of Whiteness*, eds. B. Rasmussen, E. Klinenberg, I. Nexica, & M. Wray (Durham, NC: Duke University, 2001), 44.

Deborah continues:

Why did it take almost twenty years after my friendship ended with David and Darryl for me to grieve the impact of racism? In addition to that great loss, there was witnessing the suffering of the Marshallese people as a result of colonization and the damage to my own and other white people's psyches regarding the costs of racism. What was going on in my world that led me to suppress my feelings of grief about racism? And then why, when I did experience these feelings, did I not trust them as authentic?

In retrospect, I think there were no spaces in my white world, no openings whatsoever, to talk, think, or feel about race. I spent the first fourteen years of my life in a predominantly white suburb in New Jersey. Our family then moved to a predominantly white, rural town in Ohio for two years, and then to a predominantly white suburb in California for another two years where I completed high school. I have no recollection of learning about the accomplishments and contributions of people of color to our nation. There was no discussion of race, racism, or white dominance in my K-12 schooling experiences or my university experience. The world I lived in did not allow for the possibility that a white girl or a white woman could feel sorrow about the loss of her friendship with two black boys and the existence of racism. When race did surface in my conversations at family gatherings or with other white people, racism was talked about in terms of how it caused suffering for people of color. We did not consider how racism had gotten into our bodies and minds and how we were perpetuating it.

The only exposure to learning about race and racism that I encountered occurred in my family when my parents sat me down for a kitchen table talk and stated that if they ever heard me use the word "nigger" that there would be hell to pay. That talk happened after David and Darryl's family moved to our neighborhood. At about that same time, *Roots* aired on TV. My parents made a point of allowing me to stay up past my bedtime to watch the entire series with them. The horrific image of a naked and terrified African woman, who had been repeatedly raped by her white captors, throwing herself overboard a slave ship to end her suffering is seared in my memory. I learned that the term "nigger" was a severe and dangerous word never to be spoken and that the Middle Passage and slavery were horrific and terrorizing experiences for African and African

American people. In retrospect, I believe these exposures rooted the horror and deep fear of racism in my body, along with unconscious guilt, sorrow, and anger about the systematic cruelty and abuse in which white people engage. I was ten years old when I saw *Roots*, and I am grateful to my parents for trusting that I was capable of understanding the inhumanity of the world in which we live. I believe that this experience supported me in opening to the suffering of others and becoming sensitive to injustice in the world around me.

In order to answer the question of why I took so long to experience my feelings of grief about the existence of racism, I must also consider the dynamics of my family. The overall message I received from my parents regarding emotion was: "Don't feel." As a child, I internalized the idea that my interior life was burdensome and unwelcome. Given this, I am not surprised that I did not challenge my parents' request to stop wrestling with David and Darryl. As an adult, I have tried to imagine myself sitting at the kitchen table with my parents as they told me I could not wrestle with David and Darryl anymore and to reconnect with what I might have felt then. Anger and confusion come up for me because my parents were taking away something warm and sweet. Wrestling with David and Darryl was fun. Being with them was a source of joy for me. While I didn't like what my parents requested, I also trusted them, though this trust was also mixed with fear. I knew that there was no place for me to express anger with my parents or to question their decisions. Anger at my parents was usually met with a larger verbal (and sometimes physical) anger that was abusive, frightening, and silencing. Consequently, I learned to avoid feeling anger, and I lost my voice and ability to be authentic and whole. I learned to distance myself from my own immediate thoughts and feelings while in my family, and I carried this way of being into my social context. This was particularly true in regards to being attuned to the presence of racism in the world around me. The cumulative impact of being in a family that denied authentic expression of emotion while living in a larger social world that did not allow intellectual or emotional space to think and feel about race led me to quietly sever a piece of my own soul. Thus, I was able to evade accountability about my participation in a system of racial dominance.

To realize that as children we were misinformed by the people whom we loved and trusted most is to become aware of a betrayal. Uncovering such experiences and our buried emotions, allowing unacknowledged grief about racism to surface, feeling shame, guilt, and the accompanying despair is part of the process of recovery for white people.

Deborah concludes:

There are layers and layers of intellectual, emotional, and spiritual work involved with wrestling with race and racism. I have worked through grief and anger that sometimes overwhelmed me. As I moved through despair, I then discovered another layer that contained shame about being white and participating in a system that has caused such profound suffering. When I slowed enough to feel the bodily discomfort of shame, I was able to transform it into forgiveness and compassion for myself. In moving through the pain that I had buried about racism—my anger, shame and grief—I have discovered a deep, warm, powerful place in myself, my humanity. It is within my own humanity that I find renewal and strength to continue to address racism in the different realms of my life.

5 | Shame

Shame is such an intense emotion. It just can drive you.

Kyra Sedgwick

Shame is crafty and insidious.

Valerie Kack-Brice, *The Emotion Handbook*

Racism is profound, and, like other forms of spiritual abuse, it harms everyone involved. The means of attempting to protect oneself from the psychological and emotional impact of witnessing such injustice are limited, and each has its cost. It is possible to actively join the perpetration and to mentally justify the behavior. People who choose that path and do not allow themselves to feel or imagine what the victims are experiencing cut themselves off from their own humanity. More frequently, perhaps, witnesses to racial abuse are conscious of the harm being done and keep silent, thus internalizing shame, guilt, and despair. When we act in demeaning ways towards others and do not offer sincere apologies, the shame that is inherent in our actions gets projected onto our victims. If the recipients of the humiliation are vulnerable, they feel and own the shame as though it truly belongs to them. If they are not conscious of this major error and do not have the resources to heal the hurt in it, the shame may become an ancestral wound to be passed on for generations. In an attempt to escape the shaming consequences of racial oppression, many people have denied their racial heritage. Although this phenomenon of "carried shame" has been frequently discussed as it applies to cases of physical, sexual, and emotional abuse, social oppression is rarely examined in this particular way. Yet, it offers profound examples, perhaps none more powerful than that of racism.

> *We went to the First Nations Museum. I walked round and round, and I finally had to get out because I couldn't stand the shame of it all.*
>
> Comment from a British visitor to Canada, overheard
> during a shuttle ride, July 2011

For generations, tribal peoples have been treated in shameful ways by those who arrived after them. Not only have millions been robbed and murdered, they have also been stripped of nearly every form of human dignity. Claiming even small amounts of Native American heritage as a source of pride is relatively new to Americans with white-skin privilege. Despite that growth and the work of tribal leaders to restore the dignity that originally belonged to their people, most Native Americans live in dire socioeconomic conditions and continue to be treated as less than equal. Even as she worked so hard to protect her children from being humiliated by the larger society, Kate's mother was neither able to protect them from the shame that she carried nor from the grief that comes with the recognition of loss.

This is Kate's story:

When I sat down to write about how racism has affected me as a white person, I was amazed at how hard it was to choose which story to share. I have experienced loss of identity and family closeness as well as loss of the richness that comes with diversity. I've also lived with shame and isolation. All because of racism. Finally, I chose to write about my mother's family secret and its effect on me.

When I was a child, I would often ask my mother "What is our nationality?" and she always responded "We are like Heinz 57 ketchup—you have a little bit of everything." No matter how much I pressured her to be more specific, she would repeat the same saying and walk away. Sometimes she would add, "It doesn't matter. We are all the same. No one is better or worse than anyone else." But, although I knew there was something that she wasn't telling me, she never answered my question. I remember being puzzled by her silence and feeling a sense of loss.

I knew that my father's mother had traveled with her family to the United States from Ireland when she was seventeen years old. My father's grandfather had been a farmer in Alsace-Lorraine and had come to this country from France with his two brothers when he was a young adult. Since I did not know my mother's heritage, I took pride in being Irish and French. Every time one of my teachers mentioned Ireland or France's history, my ears perked up. However, that only explained half my heritage and I felt a sense of sadness not knowing my full ancestry. It never dawned on me that my mother did not know her parents' ancestry until, when I was nineteen years old, she finally opened up to me.

I remember the day very clearly. We were sitting in the living room when I asked her about her ancestry for the hundredth time, and she finally admitted that she really didn't know. She said that her father (my grandfather Green) refused to talk about his heritage. He always responded to her questions by saying, "You have a little bit of everything in you." She only knew that her father was ashamed of some part of his heritage.

She also said that, since she did not know what her father was hiding, she tried to protect us eight kids from ever being exposed to bigoted remarks. She was afraid that someday we all would find out what racial group we belonged to, and she didn't want us to be hurt by that information.

Although my mother was not someone to take a stand on many issues, she stood firm on this one. According to her, two of my father's older brothers were outspoken with their prejudice against other racial groups. She told my father that if either of his two older brothers ever made a prejudicial remark in front of us kids, they would not be allowed in our house. I don't know exactly what my father said to them, but I never heard either of them utter any racist words until I was twenty-one years old. Unfortunately, when my favorite uncle openly shared his racism, a major rift between us was created. But that is another story. My mother did not discover what racial group her father was hiding until I was thirty-five years old. Her sister Bonnie had pressured my grandfather's sister into telling her. My mother said that her great-grandmother Sarah was Native American and that my great-grandmother Green (Sarah's daughter) was called a "half breed" while growing up in Kansas. That was all the information that my great-aunt would share.

I only met my great-grandmother Green once. I was ten years old, and I remember her being unhappy and distant. Upon hearing her story, I felt more compassion and sadness for her. I also felt outrage at the effects of racism on my grandfather, his mother, his grandmother, and our entire family. Instead of celebrating their rich heritage, they hid in shame to avoid being ridiculed and abused. I feel a deep loss at not knowing their stories and also at not having the Native American wisdom and spiritual beliefs passed down to me as a child. I was grateful that my mother had not raised us to believe that any race was better or less than another and I felt a lot of pride when I learned that I had Native American heritage. In my early twenties I read John G. Neihardt's book, *When the Tree Flowered: An Authentic Tale of the Old Sioux World*, a wonderful story about the rich spiritual beliefs of the Sioux people. I remember feeling an instant connection to their beliefs in only taking what they needed from the land and always giving thanks for what they took. I would love to have been raised with a deeper connection and respect for all life. I also admired their belief in not getting attached to physical possessions and giving away those for which attachment is felt. They strongly believed that we lose parts of our souls when we let our possessions matter too much.

After my mother shared this new information about our ancestry, I told my children, Aaron, age eight, and Lauren, age three, that they were part Native American. I shared how proud I felt about this part of our heritage. The next day, Aaron came home from school and gleefully told me that he had announced to his classmates that he was 90 percent Native American. When I told him that his Native ancestry was probably closer to 3 percent, he shouted "I want to be 90 percent Native American. It just isn't fair."

I wish that my grandfather and other Native American ancestors had been there to witness my son's disappointment. I will probably never know my great-great-grandmother Sarah's tribe. I feel a real sense of loss not knowing more about her life. "Sarah" was probably not even her birth name. I tried to search for her genealogy. There were many nomadic tribes living in Kansas during that period, and I possessed too little information. I do have the pride of knowing that our family moved 180 degrees from being totally ashamed to being very proud. I also feel a richer and more complete identity knowing that I am part of a resilient and spiritual people. But I can't stop thinking that if it weren't for racism. . . .

Brenda connects the terror she experienced living with physically and emotionally abusive parents with the insanity of South African apartheid. As a child, Brenda took great risks and used significant amounts of energy in a valiant effort to hold on to her own spirit and sense of integrity. Even so, her self-esteem and spirituality suffered great loss. In her poignant story, the relationship between virulent adultism and virulent racism is clear, as is her determination to free herself from both oppressions. The racial privilege and sense of entitlement that was legally authenticated by the system of apartheid in which Brenda's family lived throughout her childhood resulted in Brenda's absorbing and carrying not only her parents' shame, but also that of her entire culture.

Brenda writes:

I did not set out to rebel or to lie when I joined the Brownies. On the contrary, a Brownie's oath was all about honor, duty, and obedience. On the day I carried home my new tunic and scarf, I fully intended to live by the Brownie Promise of obedience and honor. I felt proud and brave.

As I diligently memorized the Brownie Promise "to do my best, to do my duty to God, the king, and my country, to help other people every day, and to obey the Brownie Law," I was unaware that I was about to step onto the road of duplicity and perfidy. The noble words thrilled me.

I practiced my Brownie salute, hooking my pinkie and fourth finger down with my thumb while keeping the other two fingers upright. Eventually I would be old enough to be a Girl Guide, and salute with three fingers. The day I received my Brownie badge I was shivering with anticipation, believing I would be transformed into a better person. In my hand I clutched the small badge, shaped like the three-leafed trefoil, until the brass grew warm; and even after all these years, I still have that little badge. Before I fell asleep, I wished with all my heart to honor the Brownie Law and Promise. From now on, I was going to be trustworthy, loyal, brave, and obedient.

I listened carefully to the troop leader who explained my new responsibilities. I nodded very seriously as she ticked off on her fingers, "Iron your own uniform, polish your own shoes, and, most important, shine your own Brownie badge—on *both* sides, because the Greek gods always look both at front and back." While I wasn't too sure about what the Greek gods did, I was even less sure about how to do my duty to God, king, and country. The way I saw things, God would surely be an even bigger, louder, and angrier version of my father, and from my experience with my father, I assumed that God would be just as irrational. I figured that the king part would be easier, since South Africans did not bother much about the king who lived in England. I hoped that I'd eventually discover how to do my duty to my country. Right now, however, I faced a huge challenge with all that polishing and ironing, which had always been "servants' work" in our household.

I expected that my mother might make a bit of a fuss. After all, it was servants who polished shoes and floors, and it was only Lizzie, the washwoman, who ever did the ironing. When it wasn't the day for ironing, the blankets that went onto the kitchen table, and the iron itself, were put away on the top shelf of the broom closet.

I had watched Lizzie iron. She would spread a shirt on the blankets, dip her hand into a basin of water and shake it over the front of the shirt. Next, she plugged the iron into the wall socket, letting it heat up so that it sizzled when she spat on it. Then she moved the iron back and forth, and the wrinkles disappeared.

I was afraid that it all was very complicated, but now that I was a Brownie, it was up to me to learn to iron. I knew I could not mention this, even to my sisters. I plotted and I waited, until one evening after supper when my father was relaxing in his big green chair, reading his paper and listening to his favorite program on his radio. I knew I was in luck when I heard my mother gossiping with friends on the phone. Here at last was my chance.

I held my breath as I dragged a chair to the broom closet, reaching for the blankets, which turned out to be very heavy. I wrestled them onto the high kitchen table before taking down the iron. I plugged the iron into the wall socket, and, just like Lizzie, set the iron on its heel to keep it from burning the table. By now I was starting to feel confident that I was going to be able to iron my uniform, be a good Brownie.

Without warning, my mother stormed into the kitchen, fuming, "What do you think you are doing?" She pushed me up against the edge of the table, shouting, "Are you a bloody kaffir girl? Are you making trouble for us? You start doing their work and before you can say 'Jack Robinson' they are murdering us in our beds." She was sputtering and spitting at me, while she slapped me, making my cheek sting.

Scared and confused, I tried to explain. "It's because I'm a Brownie . . . I have to iron my own uniform. Miss Bonner said. . . ." I couldn't finish because she was slapping me again. "You don't have to do whatever that fat English-woman tells you! I'll tell her what to do—she can throw you out of Brownies, that's what she can do. You just touch that iron again, I'll burn your hands so bad you will never forget it!" All the noise brought my father into the kitchen. He was already pulling off his belt, "I'll thrash the living daylight out of you," he said, not even asking what I had done before hitting me twice for good measure.

I went to bed quaking in fury and frustration. Now I would never be a good Brownie. Now I could not keep my Brownie promise. That night, as I bit my pillow in rage, outright rebellion was born, and along with the rebellion came deep shame of my parents. My mother might have thought she had intimidated me, but I resolved that from now on I was prepared to deceive and to lie if that was what I had to do to be a brave and trustworthy Brownie.

So I began to plot how to polish my shoes and shine my trefoil badge. Every night the whole family left our shoes by the kitchen door so that the old man who was our "kitchen boy" could shine them early each morning. I could see no way to change this, so I resolved not to get my shoes dirty, so that he would have less work to do. At school, I walked very carefully, trying to avoid puddles or anything that would scuff the heavy black lace-up school shoes. Immediately after I got off the school bus, I took my shoes off and used my socks to wipe the shoes clean. As I carried those ugly cumbersome lace-ups all the way up uphill to our house, the hot pavement burned my feet. Even greater than the pain in my feet was the hurt in my heart from fear and despair at my parents' spiteful attitude to the people who were our servants.

Each week at Brownies, I got a stomachache as I nodded mutely when the pack leader asked us if we had ironed our own uniforms and shined our own shoes. My throat got tight and I would avoid her eyes. I knew I was lying and—even worse—I knew that she knew I was a liar. Each week, I expected to get expelled from the pack for lying, because dishonesty was even worse than not doing our duty. I knew I was neither trustworthy nor obedient. By telling so many lies I betrayed my duty to God and my country. This troubled and confused me, since I thought it was because of my country that my parents were so evil and wicked that I could not respect them. There was no one I could talk to, especially not my pack leader. I just waited every week, expecting to be told to hand back my shiny brass trefoil badge.

How I kept my precious badge so very shiny, front and back, was a secret I kept for many years. Each week, on the night before the pack meeting, I would stay awake until my sisters and my parents had gone to bed. It was hard not to fall asleep, so I told myself stories about Brownies who were brave and free to do whatever they wanted. When I thought it was safe, I moved very quietly in the dark, avoiding squeaky floor boards and creaky door hinges. I would creep into the kitchen to the cleaning cupboard in the corner. Shivering with fear that my mother might come, I crouched on the floor, working quickly in the glow of a street light. I smeared polish onto the badge, front and back, before creeping back to my bed. Once safely under the covers, I would use my school handkerchief to rub, rub, rub my badge so that it shined, front and back.

I polished that badge so often and so hard that over the years I wore away its distinctive markings. I was proud that my badge was so shiny, but it was a sad kind of pride. All my life I would know that I had betrayed my promise to do my best. Instead, I had become a sneak and a liar.

Jeffrey still carries shame when he recalls early memories. His story illustrates that even when individual white people are not actively perpetuating mistreatment, they continue to remain part of an invisible system of racism that maintains their privilege at the expense of people of color.

This is Jeffrey's story:

I grew up in a New England town of approximately nine hundred people. I knew of only one African American family there, an elderly woman and her adult grandson. There were no Asian, Jewish, Middle Eastern or Latino families. My parents taught my brother and me that discriminating against minorities was unfair, dishonest, and a form of bullying. We were taught to refer to African Americans as "colored people" or "Negroes," acceptable terms at the time. We understood that those who used crude, offensive terms were either bigoted or insensitive and ignorant.

I attended a regional high school of about 160 students, all of whom were white. I was active in sports and played against teams from nearby towns, several of which had African American players. There was the normal schoolboy rivalry between the teams, but I never observed any racial animosity among the players.

Our family had no African American friends. Then again, we had no Latino, Jewish, Middle-Eastern or Asian friends. I didn't think it unusual—if I thought about it at all. There was no one from those groups around. The de facto segregation I grew up with was invisible to me.

In 1957, my last year of high school, my senior class capped the year by making a trip to Washington, D.C. The itinerary included a stay in New York City and a side trip to Colonial Williamsburg in Virginia. I was a small-town boy and, frankly, I was more interested in spending my time exploring the big cities of Washington and New York. In the course of my school years I'd taken "educational" class trips to historical sites in Boston, New Bedford, Plymouth, and Sturbridge, Massachusetts. There we saw the early years of America recreated through exhibits and reenactments. I thought the trips were a pleasant relief from day-to-day schoolwork but not much more than that. I felt Williamsburg would be the same. I was in for a surprise.

Soon after we arrived at Colonial Williamsburg, I came across the signs above the drinking fountains: "White" and "Colored." The sight shocked me, and the memory of it still resonates. For some reason I'd thought of Virginia as being more enlightened than the white-sheeted South of George Wallace and Bull Connor that I'd read about and seen on TV. Uh-uh. The message those signs sent was as gut-level ugly as seeing an adult strike a child. A police officer stood near the fountains, and one of my classmates asked him about the unusual, single handcuff he had on his belt. It had a pistol grip and the man explained that it was used to subdue a person. He clicked it several times to show how it could tighten. "If someone resisted," he said, "it could break his bones."

Looking back now, it seems likely that the officer was guarding the general area, not the fountains in particular. But I still have the visceral feeling of seeing brutality and injustice linked. It struck me as odd that an attraction meant to highlight American ideals should be a showcase for the country's dark side. The Cold War was in full bloom then, and the United States was in a propaganda battle with the Soviet Union. Even though I hailed from the North, I believed that the South was still part of our country. The Williamsburg display was touted as an international tourist attraction. Was it really the image that we wanted to present to the world?

In my sophomore year of college, I was having difficulties and took a leave of absence from school. There was military conscription at that time, and I knew I'd be drafted once I was no longer a student. I decided to enlist and get it over with. After basic training in New Jersey, I was sent to Fort Benning, Georgia, where I was assigned to an infantry battalion as a rifleman. I spent a few days in a replacement center, waiting to be processed into my new unit. As I sweltered in the muggy July heat, I realized I'd soon be tramping the dusty trails and running up and down the red dirt hills of Georgia in full combat gear. It was a depressing thought. Fortunately, when I was processing through the personnel section, the sergeant in charge noticed I had a year-and-a-half of college and had done well on my army entrance tests. He offered me a job as clerk in his section, which I eagerly accepted.

There was no enlisted men's club near our battalion, but there was a small Post Exchange nearby that had an outdoor patio where they served 3.2 beer. It was better than nothing, if only slightly. There I met an African American soldier from Brooklyn who was assigned to one of the infantry companies in my battalion. We became friends and would meet at the PX and talk about music, films, and books. And, of course, we'd gripe about the army. Our friendship was restricted, though, confined to base. There was no official racial discrimination at Fort Benning because a dozen years earlier President Truman had integrated the army. But once we stepped off the base into the neighboring city of Columbus, segregation was the law of the land. There, my friend and I weren't allowed to go to movies, clubs, or restaurants together, nor could we even sit together on public transportation.

In the course of our conversations at the PX, I learned that my friend had earned a master's degree in chemistry from Long Island University. Following that, he'd been drafted. After basic training, he was assigned to my battalion as a rifleman, the job I'd lucked out of. He'd passed through the same personnel center I had, but he hadn't been so lucky.

So how did it happen that an intelligent guy with a master's degree in chemistry was running hills while a college dropout was working as a desk jockey? My friend and I never discussed the question. The answer was painfully obvious.

I recently told an old friend about the revulsion I'd felt in Virginia and the guilt I'd felt in Georgia. He suggested that in the first case it was more than revulsion, it was a form of shame. I hadn't put up the signs above the water fountains, but in a sense they were put up in my name. After all, the people of Virginia were my countrymen. Although mine wasn't the shame of the doer, it was the shame you feel when a member of your family does something disgraceful. He also suggested that what I felt about my favorable re-assignment at Fort Benning was more shame than guilt. My friend at Fort Benning had been denied the consideration I'd received simply because of the color of his skin. I felt the shame that a favored child feels when he gets better treatment than his siblings.

More than half a century later, I still feel ill at ease when I recall those events.

One of the ways that humans choose to relieve themselves of shame and to feel better about themselves for a short period of time is to project that shame onto others. Sometimes the shame is projected onto an entire race of people. Ann tells a story about one of her white students during her years as a college instructor.

During the 1970s, I taught a course called "Ethnic Group Relations" to college students. One of the white students came to each session of the class but did not participate in any way, sitting as far away as possible from his African American classmates, with his arms folded across his chest. At the end of the semester, he came to my office distraught because he had failed the class and begged me to give him a C so that he could continue to play football.

I listened to him and then told him that he needed to do a homework assignment in order to earn a C-. His assignment was to write a paper that focused on his thoughts about black people and to begin each sentence with "They."

The next day, he brought the paper to my office. It was three pages long and contained sentence after sentence about black people and the changes he perceived them making. Examples: "They used to be happy, but now they are angry. They used to dance, and now they want to fight. They used to like me, but now they hate me." On and on it went in that way.

I read the paper and told him he had to do one more thing. He was to sit at my desk and rewrite the paper in almost the same way. The one change he had to make was to change each sentence so that "I" was substituted for "They."

Examples: "I used to be happy, but now I am angry. I used to dance and now I want to fight. I used to like me, but now I hate me."

He did the assignment and in the midst of it, the truth of the personal statements hit him and he began to sob. He cried and cried and when he was done, he talked about his family and his relationship with his father whom he saw as harsh and impossible to please. Until that moment, in his denial of his own feelings, he had projected his damaged self-esteem and his anger and shame onto all African Americans. With his tearful release and increased self-awareness, he was finally on a path toward freedom from racism.

Eilene's anxiety about not being able to recognize a Latina employee is an excellent example of how fear gets in the way of clear thinking in cross-racial relationships. This experience led her to a place of questioning herself and feeling her own shame. In that way, she, too, opened a doorway to personal healing.

For several years, I hired Rosa to clean our home every two weeks. She had moved from Mexico to the United States and was not completely comfortable speaking English. However, although my Spanish is very limited, we were able to communicate enough to take care of the necessities. If we took our time, we could also talk a little about our children and health issues and occasionally about fun things like hairstyles! We were about the same age and I was grateful for her help with our house. She definitely made my life easier. I also liked her and looked forward to seeing her.

In addition to her freelance housekeeping work, Rosa worked as a maid at a local hotel. I became aware that when I asked her "How was your Mother's Day?" or "Did you have a nice Easter?" she was most likely going to tell me that she worked on that day. That was a good reminder that time off for rest and connection with one's family is a privilege (although it seems to me it should be a right).

Sometimes, Rosa brought one of her daughters or other family members to work with her. Her daughters spoke fluent English and would often translate between Rosa and me. I had a friendly relationship with one of her daughters in particular and would ask her about Rosa's grandchildren.

When Rosa had surgery to correct back problems, she was not able to work for a couple of months. During that time, other members of her family continued to clean our house. One housecleaning day, I came out of our front door as one of the women pulled up in front of the house. She got out of her car and started unloading the cleaning supplies. As we greeted each other, I realized with shock that I had no idea what her name was. I knew that this woman had been in my house many times and that she and I had talked several times. We had certainly been introduced. Was she one of Rosa's daughters? Her niece? Could it be Rosa herself? I could not bring myself to ask her name. I kept smiling and making small talk, pretending that I knew exactly who she was.

Was it possible that after all the contact, all the conversations, and all the warm friendly feelings, that I could not see these Latinas as individuals? Did blocking out individual identities make it easier for me to take advantage of their service? I felt deeply ashamed.

Diana writes: "I still feel shame about my automatic racist thoughts" and shares several vignettes related to the family experiences that instilled them. Her stories are indicative of how early teachings can stay with us, even when we have rejected them in our effort to think differently.

These are Diana's stories:

My high school class president senior year was black. It's odd that this is notable . . . just like it has been notable other times when a successful person has Mexican heritage or is black. I'm ashamed that there are times when I still have that initial reaction. It takes a long time to dissipate these ingrained messages and judgments. Contributing to this book is helping me feel less guilty and ashamed for my lingering racist legacy. I know I'm not alone in facing, acknowledging, and forgiving myself.

■ ■ ■

I was always extremely uncomfortable with my mother's name for Brazil nuts. Over time, as I grew up, I found it progressively more disgusting and degrading to black people. I was more and more grossed out by my mother using that name. At some point I finally asked my mother what the other name for it was, and she was baffled. She said she had never heard them called by any other name. It was not until I was in my forties or fifties that I ever heard the proper name. I still feel ashamed that the first name that comes to mind when I see or think of Brazil nuts is a racial slur.

■ ■ ■

When I was a teenager, I began to question more of what my family said re- garding politics and race, among other issues. When someone would make a general statement of criticism about Jews or blacks or Mexicans, I would chal- lenge them, saying that not all Jews were dishonest and greedy and that not all blacks were lazy or violent. Sometimes my mother or stepfather would counter, "That's true. Johnny at the plant is one of our hardest workers." Sometimes the response was overstated, similar to the old "One of my good friends is a black man."

I felt hurt and shame for the racist comments and the overcompensa- tions. I especially lost more respect for my stepfather, as he was the greatest perpetrator. The positive effect was that I began to trust my own judgment and opinions more.

■   ■   ■

In 1967 I went to Fort Benning, Georgia, from Wisconsin with my newlywed first husband for his infantry officer basic training. Although my home town of Racine, Wisconsin, was predominately white and racism existed, I was not pre- pared for the more blatant public racism I encountered in the South.

The first time I took a public bus in Georgia, I was stunned to see the clear demarcation of the racial lines on the bus. I paused to decide where I would sit. As I walked toward the rear of the bus, the driver and white people told me I had better sit up front with my own kind. Even some black people told me I should sit up front. I stubbornly sat near the rear. I think I held my tears until I got off the bus. I couldn't believe that racism still existed in 1967. (What did I think I grew up with in Wisconsin? It was just less obvious at home.) I was shocked, in disbelief, hurt, confused, and angry.

I think the bathrooms and drinking fountains I later encountered hit me harder. I was so appalled and grossed out by the lingering segregation labels. I thought of the children being faced with it each day at school or in a park. My eyes still well up with tears as I recall my first images of segregated bathrooms.

I can't even begin to imagine what it must have been like for children of color to grow up with such demeaning reminders. My heart still breaks when I think about how cruel and unjust racism is.

In 1967, I felt ashamed of my country and angry at the South for their prejudice. It took longer for me to realize that what Northerners thought and spoke behind closed doors was all part of it too.

While in Georgia that summer of 1967, I became friends with my female neighbor who had an infant. I was very fond of this sweet woman and her darling baby. However, my contact with her husband was not comfortable at all. It became clear very soon that he was blatantly racist, loud, argumentative, and that he yelled at his wife and child a great deal. I feared what else went on. I had never heard anyone be so openly and cruelly prejudiced. He seemed to flaunt his racism and get great satisfaction out of it. Maybe, looking back, he was enjoying upsetting and shocking me. Unfortunately, I ended up seeing less of his sweet wife and child, and I developed my own temporary prejudice against people from Florida.

Despite all that she has done to rid herself of racism, Valerie, like Diana, still struggles with remnants of racist conditioning and the emotions that accompany that struggle.

Valerie shares:

Shame wells up in me as I make awkward attempts to heal around experiences with racism. I have had to consider how my entitlement rears its ugly head and how I make certain one-sided assumptions about what should happen, how I should be treated, and how someone else should act. I have felt guilty when I've become aware of ways in which I perpetrated the sickness. I think about assumptions I've made when I've seen a dark man walking with a brown paper bag or a lovely African American or Hispanic family I would like to know but can't because of the gaping divide caused by my cultural shame and my inability to cross it. I wonder why they would want to know me, a member of the oppressor race. At times, I even forget that my best friend is black because I feel so "at one" with her. While I am frequently oblivious to racial difference, racism is a painful and relentless concern for her. Sometimes, in my isolation from the grief and hopelessness that so many people of color live with, I forget that I am white and what that might mean.

Paula's decision to marry an African American man has allowed her opportunities to examine racism on a very personal level. Her insistence on being her own person, her love for her husband, and her commitment to her marriage resonate throughout her story. Still, there is sadness, anger, and an accompanying powerlessness and shame.

This is Paula's story:

I grew up on a farm outside of Abilene, Kansas. My parents were both college educated. My mother encouraged curiosity and an interest in other cultures. She was from the east coast, and she was interested in differences. She sang me Negro spirituals when I was little. She told me that she learned them, as a little girl, from the black workers who were building something close to her house. She would listen to them sing and imitate them.

If there was someone from another culture in our community, they were frequently invited to our home. I was the child who was most interested. Differences fascinated me, and I was drawn to them. I have very little interest in sameness. I am not attracted to living in a gated upper-class community. The sameness of everyone feels too restrictive, and I actually find it distasteful. I've never liked being restricted.

Freedom is one of my core values. Many times, I've exercised that freedom under the radar screen. I've shied away from public roles, as I haven't handled criticism well. I figure that, if no one knows what I am doing, I won't come under scrutiny. That may come from living in a small town and everyone knowing or thinking they know your business and wanting you to live by their rules and values. That never worked for me. I have a willingness to follow my own path, I guess. I've normally had the courage to take action when I wanted to. Typically, I will do what I want sooner rather than later.

The first time I had a black man as a friend, I was living in western Kansas. It was my first personal experience with discrimination. I knew a lot of people on the college campus because I worked in the cafeteria at the largest men's dorm. Several men stopped talking to me after seeing me with my friend.

Now, I am married to LaRhue, a black man, and I have seen, first-hand, that people are scared of young black men—even of older black men. LaRhue laughs at the looks people give him when he opens the door and they're looking for my neighbor who is a dog groomer. He says the fear in some people's eyes is funny. They look like a deer in the headlights. Recently, he told me the story of being in the parking lot of Whole Foods and walking toward an older woman. Even though he was dressed in a shirt and tie, she immediately clutched her purse and jumped out of the way. When I heard that story, I felt sadness. I tried to imagine myself in a situation where people would routinely be scared of me.

When we first got together, LaRhue told me that he has to make others comfortable within thirty seconds of meeting them or the opportunity is missed. I work at helping people feel comfortable with me also, but not because I think they're scared of me. I guess I do it because it makes me more comfortable and I want to be able to connect with them. I realize that many whites don't see black men as human beings like them. They see a bunch of stereotypes and project them.

Recently, just after arriving in Hawaii, I was in the car at a gas station trying to read the map while LaRhue was outside smoking a cigar. It wasn't more than a few minutes before the owner of the station walked out to see what he was doing. Another woman walked out and looked at him suspiciously. Had I been the one standing outside, I don't think either of them would have behaved that way. I wonder how that constant suspicion shapes one's life and what it feels like to have people looking at you like you're a menace for no reason other than the color of your skin. My best guess is that I'd feel hurt, angry, boxed in, like a victim—like no one was going to give me a chance. It would probably make me cautious because when people are scared of you, you don't know what they'll do. At times, I might feel powerful.

LaRhue used to work in the federal prison system as a drug and alcohol counselor. One day, one of the inmates, a very large and heavy-muscled black man was giving a white staff member a semi-hard time. LaRhue walked up to the inmate and told him to come to his office. He said, "Stop scaring all these white people and come to my office." He told me that the guy smiled at him because LaRhue had called him on his behavior. So at times, you could use it to your advantage—if you needed to.

Still, I see that LaRhue has a lot tougher time in life than I do. Everything is harder. Just as his skin color makes people attribute certain characteristics to him, how I look makes people attribute things to me. He has a small business where he makes sales to both individuals and small businesses. I think people here don't trust him easily and that affects his business. People always trust me. I've had a lot of opportunities because of how I look that I don't believe I would have gotten had I had black skin. I know I'm privileged.

When LaRhue and I were first together, I did not want to give up my privileges by marrying him. I knew that our relationship wasn't strong enough to deal with the multiple losses that I would experience. I was my father's favorite, and he told me he would disown me. We did not marry at that time. LaRhue and I reconnected 25 years later. By that point my father had advanced Alzheimers. LaRhue ended up helping to care for him. LaRhue shared that when we went back to see my father he was nervous and thought it ironic that he'd be put in a position to care for someone who had rejected him. My father was very docile and loving at that point and looked at LaRhue with curiousity, but that was all.

I didn't like the way people looked at me when we were out in public in conservative areas of the country. I still don't. We just don't have to deal with it very often any more. We seldom go back to the Midwest, and when we do, it's only to spend time with family. Additionally, I just don't care as much anymore about what other people think of me. Also, things have changed a lot in the past thirty years regarding interracial couples. When LaRhue and I first dated in 1976, it was only nine years after the Supreme Court ruled on the Loving case, overturning all legal restrictions on interracial marriage in the United States.

I often wonder if LaRhue and I had children how I would feel about what they would face as black teenagers. That question is the toughest for me. I couldn't ignore the mini-slights that might happen to them because that would hurt and shape them. I'd be careful about where we lived. I'd want to protect my children, especially if we had a son. A few weeks ago, I read *American Family: Things Racial* by Stacy Cusulos and Barbara Waugh. The many issues they faced raising their children and the subtle and not-so-subtle racism they faced, even living in liberal Santa Cruz, California, shocked me.

It shames me that we judge people by their skin color.

Elaine shares a few short stories on lessons learned about racism. Her identity as a Jew has been helpful in her understanding of the impact of mistreatment based on race. She tells a story of being mistreated because of anti-Semitism, as well as stories of witnessing mistreatment due to racism. These shameful experiences resulted in an examination of her own behavior. She has been able to recognize that her ignorance and lack of understanding are consequences of racist conditioning. In the process of helping others, she is able to continue her own growth.

This is Elaine's story:

I grew up in a small New England city, in a civil society where good manners mattered. There were only two or three African Americans in our high school, and prejudice was silently expressed, so far as I knew. Discrimination was shown quietly towards those whose difference was invisible, like us Jewish kids. There were the clubs that we weren't asked to join and parties that we didn't get invited to, but I don't remember anyone being called names or experiencing outright cruelty. I also don't remember being unhappy about it or thinking about being left out, mostly because we had a strong sense of belonging in our own community.

In reply to the question of how racism has affected me, I have to go back to my sophomore year of college. In the many years since then, the profoundness of suddenly gaining some understanding of what bigotry feels like lingers.

During the spring of 1960, I was dating a boy from the gentile fraternity house next door to my dorm. He was a great guy and I was such a "good girl." When it came time for the annual spring weekend when the fraternity rented a house on Cape Cod for three days of what passed for debauchery in those days, he knew better than to invite me. One Saturday night before the big event, while we were sitting around with a group of other kids, his roommate asked him whom he was taking to the spring weekend. Probably fearing that his manhood might come into question, my boyfriend answered that he was thinking about "picking up a hot-blooded black from South Boston." His roommate came over to me, lifted my arm as if for inspection and said, "She's not much better." The coarseness, the ignorance, and the malice were appalling. I don't remember the hurt as much as the embarrassment and shame that I felt for them.

To continue searching for an answer to how racial prejudice has affected me as a white person, I need to refer to other experiences.

One occurred when my husband was serving overseas as an U.S. Army medical officer. We lived on base and I was part of the Officers' Wives Club. For a program at one of our meetings, I invited an artist to show her paintings. Her work was beautiful and the two small paintings that I bought from her that day still hang in our house. But as we left the building together, this lovely, talented, intelligent young black woman turned to me with tears in her eyes and said "They wouldn't talk to me."

"Who wouldn't?" I incredulously asked.

"None of them," she answered. I don't know how I reacted. I don't remember what I said and can only hope that it was something kind and reasonable. Was I the ignorant one? Maybe I didn't even say to anyone that our presenter would be an African American. Why would I? Was I culpable for being unaware of the prejudices of the other women who found it necessary to snub a visitor? Did innocence make me guilty? Once again, I was ashamed for them and for myself, that I didn't know better than to put her in such a position.

I also want to tell a story about something that happened years later. My longtime friend, Gladys, was originally from Jamaica and had two sons close in age to our children. We often babysat for one another, even leaving our kids overnight with each other. After one such event, when she had stayed at our house while my husband and I were on vacation, she came to me with a tale that brought tears to both of us. It seems that our fourteen-year-old son had asked her if he could bring a school friend home. She told him that was fine, but in telling me about it wept, "He never said that his friend was black, too."

Then, at that stage of maturity, I knew that it was right to put my arms around her. As we hugged each other I said a silent thanks. Our children had not learned prejudice in their home from their parents. I am so grateful.

As a psychotherapist, I have had the opportunity to train as a leader for race relations study circles. Perhaps, in the end, racism has pushed me to gain in understanding and to attempt to help others to grow. It is a gift to be able to give back, to show in some small way that there are people of good will who care.

6   Silence

In the context of the Negro problem neither whites nor blacks, for excellent reasons of their own, have the faintest desire to look back; but I think that the past is all that makes the present coherent, and further, that the past will remain horrible for exactly as long as we refuse to assess it honestly.

James Baldwin, *Notes of a Native Son*

I was taught to see racism only in individual acts of meanness by members of my group, never in invisible systems conferring unsought racial dominance on my group from birth.

Peggy McIntosh, 1988

Seeing what is invisible and naming it is extremely difficult. One of the ways in which white Americans have been damaged by racism is the conditioning to be blind to ways in which they benefit from the current political and economic system. When conversations about race take place in groups that are racially diverse, white people often feel personally blamed for racism. They then become defensive, hearing verbal exchange as a personal attack rather than a conversation about the system that we all share. Caroline relates some of her observations about facilitating dialogues on race in a university setting.

Caroline's thoughts:

I have been teaching courses on diversity, multiculturalism, and oppression for almost twenty years. I have had the opportunity to witness behavior that is conditioned and repetitive, particularly among white people. Recently, on the first day of teaching a two-day course for university faculty and staff with my colleague, an African American woman, we facilitated an emotionally charged conversation about race relations in the United States. That type of conversation happens often as we work with a group of people from different backgrounds in dynamic study of content related to diversity.

On the second day of training, one of the white trainees shared her fear of participating in the heated conversation that had occurred on the previous day. Because of her discomfort with the verbal interactions, she made the decision to keep her mouth shut, she said, for fear that a person of color would get upset with what she said. I let her know of my appreciation for her willingness to speak up and her honesty in letting the group know what had been going on for her during the time when she had chosen to remain silent. I then asked her if she was willing for me to comment about what she had said. She agreed. I pointed out that while it was scary for her to open her mouth and share what she thought because she did not want the discomfort of someone either challenging her or disagreeing with what she had to say, the truth was that people of color have to live their lives in fear everyday of being mistreated, oppressed, threatened or even annihilated, just for being themselves. I asked her if she could see the irony in that juxtaposition of realities. White people refuse to have conversations with people of color about how racism really affects their daily lives for fear of discomfort; people of color have to be subjected to mistreatment and the possibility of violence due to racism every day.

Standing up and speaking out about racism is necessary for change to occur. If we keep silent about the ways in which groups of people are dehumanized, the system remains in place. Compassion and forgiveness are critical however, when examining our own behavior and the ways in which we have remained silent. When we are able to forgive ourselves and make new decisions about speaking up, we reduce the shame, guilt, and feelings of powerless that support the continuation of injustice. Leon still experiences shame when he recalls witnessing an act of oppression and remaining silent about the mistreatment.

Leon explains:

My heart hurts and I experience shame when I think of my own experiences colluding with oppressive behavior.

"No room in the hotel" says the manager of the Narragansett Hotel in Kennebunkport Beach to an obviously Jewish couple seeking a room for the night.

There were rooms . . . and I was the silent bellhop.

Louise's story focuses on memories of her mother's racist conditioning, the shame it created for her, and the challenge to move out of silence.

This is Louise's story:

After her death, and influenced by an African American friend whose family history and civil rights quest caused me to wonder about my southern roots, I thought of my mother.

She liked to visit.

She liked to visit me to see the many places where I lived so that she could "picture my home in (her) mind." She liked adventure. I guess that's how, in 1936, she ended up in a small Wisconsin town of five hundred Polish and Norwegian people who still spoke their native languages. She had grown up in the South and was trying to fit in after moving there with her husband (my father), who was starting a medical practice.

Growing up in North Carolina, my mother was two years old when her father and his brother, both medical doctors, died of tuberculosis. "They got it from a stable hand," she said. "He was helping them mount their horses." As she told this story, embellishing it year after year, I came to realize that this man must have been black. I also think that my mother must have had an

African American cook, since another frequently repeated family story was that my father taught my mother to cook because she couldn't cook when they got married.

My parents left Virginia, where they had attended the medical college, to find a small country town in his native Wisconsin. My mother was terribly homesick, so we'd fly, drive, or take the train to visit her relatives.

"Don't point," she would say when we traveled to Richmond, warning me that I'd be "seeing Negroes, and it isn't nice to point." There was never any discussion about the separate drinking fountains.

I remember how elegant and stylish some of the black women were, walking on the old brick streets of Richmond with their matching high heels, hats, gloves and hand bags. I had never seen anything like that where I lived. I would point, trying to get my mother's attention. I realize now that she did not want me embarrassing her. Later in life, she said things like, "Why do they have to drive those big cars?" In my thirties, I began answering, "Because they can't buy a house in a neighborhood they'd like to live in!" Clearly my mother was uncomfortable.

She was always critical of people who were very different from her and instilled that tendency in me. It has taken years for me to diminish the legacy I was given, and I feel shame when I examine her racist conditioning. Her parting comment regarding race was said one brilliant summer day in Carmel, California.

On one of her adventures, she had come for a visit. We were walking up the hill from the village on a warm sunny day, past quaint cottages with colorful gardens of pink geraniums. We came up behind a friend of mine dressed in a summer shift and sandals. Walking some distance behind her, my mother said, "She's a Negro. I can tell by her heels." Embarrassed, I froze. I couldn't recover fast enough to introduce her to my friend. We continued to walk behind her at a distance. I kept the secret of the comment for over thirty years. A discussion about my contributing to this book released the story. Now I wonder: How was I any different from my mother? I was never able to talk with her about the incident and I never introduced her to my friend.

It is very important for me to think that, by now, I have gained enough courage to speak out against racism.

Diana relates her memories and writes of times when she wishes she had been able to speak out against the injustice she witnessed. This type of self-examination is essential for white people in order to heal and become better allies to people of color, as well as to preserve their own humanity. Although Diana does not speak of personal courage as she shares the alliance with her high school acquaintance, she risked being ostracized by other classmates as she reached out to that young woman. In so doing, she demonstrated strength and integrity. Her memories of her history teacher reflect some of the powerlessness that young people feel when witnessing and experiencing racism and adultism.

Diana writes:

In one high school study hall, I got to know a white girl who was known to date black fellas. It seemed like most white kids avoided her. I talked with her, and she seemed friendly and pleasant. As we talked more, she opened up and told me how isolated she felt. She was being rejected by whites, she said, and not fully accepted or trusted by blacks either. Black girls were jealous and felt she was stealing their guys away.

She said she didn't know or understand why she was attracted to black men, but she was. Also, she said that now that she had gone out with black men, none of the white guys would accept her. Unfortunately, she had been chastised by her family as well.

She usually looked so hunched over and dejected. I felt really bad for her and was amazed at how she lit up when I engaged with her. She was interesting and smarter than I had assumed. When we spoke, she felt accepted and not judged. I enjoyed that semester of getting to know her in study hall and I discovered that this "castaway" was a sweet, kind, and sensitive young woman.

■　■　■

I had a memorable American history teacher. I wish I could say that on the day John F. Kennedy was assassinated, Dr. Ping Chu let us leave history class for the television news in the student union, or to deal with our grief, or to discuss what was happening as living history in the making. However, he droned on with his boring version of dead American history.

That was not the only reason he was memorable. His worst crimes were against the black culture. He loved having discussions about slavery and the civil war, dogmatically claiming that blacks and Africans were inferior and, according to science, had smaller brains. I think our class textbook even agreed with this person called a "professor." One day he was so harsh and cruel that the only young black woman in our class broke down and ran out of the classroom sobbing. I felt so sad and pained for her, and so disgusted and angry with the teacher. I wish now that I had had the maturity to go after her and comfort her or to confront him and report him.

Even though I was not yet evolved enough to take action, I realize now as I write this, that it was one of many painful experiences in life that contributed to my developing compassion and empathy for others and which led to my becoming a psychologist.

A few years ago, Ann had a painful experience with a group of white friends who were silent while they listened to one woman tell a graphic story about her husband's overt racism, never asking Ann how listening to the story affected her as an African American woman. Ann decided to speak to them about their silence and to also work harder at figuring out unconscious racism. Having had many experiences facilitating diversity workshops with Sue, a white friend who was not part of that experience, Ann asked her for input. This was Sue's response.

Sue's thoughts:

You asked me to write down some of my thoughts about white racism (mine in particular).

What I'm figuring out (in a deeper way) is that there's no way for me not to make mistakes. (Damn!) As a white person, my racist conditioning is so thorough that it seeps out of my pores. I have a lot of good information, and I've learned to do/say or not do/say certain things that are racist and hurtful. But I don't know what I don't know. And no amount of being "careful" (which is my specialty) will completely prevent me from sometimes acting out my racism on people of color. So the skills of "Whoops!" and "tell me more [about how I've been racist towards you]" are obviously of primary importance for me to hone. Of course, the other antidote for what I don't know I don't know is to continue to make sure I'm getting the thinking of people of color who can see things I can't yet see.

We know that white people will have to support each other in order to end racism. That means not dividing ourselves into "the bad ones" and "the good ones."

My chronic pattern of being a "good girl" makes that hard for me. The two keys to being a "good girl" are 1) to behave reasonably well, be vigilant, considerate, kind, thoughtful, bright and pretty, and 2) (most important) to not get caught when you don't achieve number one.

A part of me is pulled (hard) to be a "good white person"—or, for God's sake, at least not to be found out when I'm not! I trust that you can picture how desperate I feel to be seen that way.

The other key piece for me is looking at how working- and middle-class oppression has shaped my racism. The message that got engraved on my "record" was that every person is supposed to achieve financial and material success and comfort. If you don't "make it," it's because something is wrong with you. And if that's the case, it is deeply shameful, and should be hidden at all costs. Since my family struggled with "making it" as well as hiding the struggle, that one is in there pretty deep.

As a young person, I noticed that people of color appeared to be struggling. While my fresh young person's intelligence told me that this was terrible injustice and certainly no fault of the people being targeted, I also had to reconcile that with the misinformation of class oppression, which was incessantly promoted in my family (two generations of disappointed middle-class women married to working-class men) and everywhere else I looked.

So far, from the work I have done with white people on healing from our racist conditioning, I believe my patterns are representative of a lot of white people with similar backgrounds to mine. (The variations are wherever the chronic distress lies with that particular white person.) We do so desperately want to be seen as good people. More important: we want to believe we are good people.

Once during a workshop on healing the wounds of oppression, a Latina, who was new to the group and whom I had met only briefly, came up to hug me, with a warm and open smile on her face. She sat next to me during the demonstrations, her body shaking as she listened. When the leaders asked for feedback, this woman said that although it was indeed hard to hear these "records" of racism and classism, she felt encouraged and appreciative of the white people who took the risk to put them out. I am reminded how much my sisters and brothers of color are rooting for us white people, how many times a day a person of color must make the decision to forgive and be generous to a white person.

I am also reminded of how firmly my own liberation is entwined with the liberation of people of color. As long as racism holds people of color down, we white people occupy a position of unearned privilege. It skews our view of reality, and makes us call into question (consciously or unconsciously) our true worth. It divides us from one another and makes us distrustful of each other and ourselves. It pollutes our thinking about and relationships with the majority of people in the world with fear and confusion, or it has us invest them with super-human purity and strength.

I hope this helps to paint the picture of "What the hell goes on with white people, anyway?" I also know that people of color know much more about us than we know about ourselves. Thanks for asking.

Sue continues to explore her own challenges as they relate to the impact of racism in her life.

Sue writes:

Several years ago I attended a weekend leadership conference with a racially diverse group of about sixty people. At one point the workshop leader urged white people to take action to interrupt racism when we see it. He stressed that interrupting racism is so critical that it is more important to take action than to worry about hurting a white person's feelings or getting it exactly right. Many of us white participants were inspired by the leader's words.

Shortly afterwards, I met with my small learning group of about six white people. One of the men in the group, Eddie, talked about his resolution to act on the leader's direction. He said he wanted to make a closer connection with one of the African American men in the large group. He planned to sit down with the black man and tell him all the things that he (Eddie) had figured out about racism. The other small group members and the facilitator of the small group gave Eddie appreciation for his courage and thinking and warmly encouraged him to go for it. I was silent. Eddie's plan struck me as being "off." The most basic tenet of "allyship" is that people who experience oppression are the experts on that oppression. Rather than a white person telling an African American about racism, wouldn't it be more appropriate for the white person to listen to the African American's experiences? It sounded to me like the potential for one more unaware racist annoyance perpetrated on a black person and a set-up for both men.

I wasn't sure what to do. I felt strongly that Eddie's plan was counterproductive, but it was confusing to me that no one else, not the small group facilitator, not the other group members, nor Eddie himself, saw anything wrong with it.

I didn't know anyone well at the conference. Little by little I had been making connections with some of the participants. Because of some things that were going on in my life at that time, reaching out to men seemed particularly challenging to me. Eddie and I had already made a nice connection in the small group and spent some time talking together. I liked him and thought he was a good guy.

The next morning, I found Eddie in the breakfast buffet line and asked to talk with him. We both got our food and sat down at a table. I was shaking. I plunged in and told him about my concerns. His smile faded and his body stiffened. He seemed angry. When I finished speaking, he picked up his breakfast without saying a word, got up, and moved to another table. He avoided me for the rest of the weekend.

I believe my thinking was good, but I felt awful for not being able to make him understand without hurting his feelings. I don't know if he went through with his plan . . . if what I said made sense to him and he changed his approach to getting close to the African American man, or if he was discouraged from taking any positive action.

I wish I had the chance for a "do-over." At that conference, I did the best I could. It seemed better to do something that wasn't perfect than to do nothing. Today, I can think of more effective ways that I might have approached Eddie, including showing my interest in hearing his thoughts about racism, and then suggesting that we think together about how both of us could be better allies to people of color.

This is one of the ways that racism divides us white people from one another. Any hint of criticism around racism, the slightest implication that we think the other white person is racist, can generate hurt, anger, and defensiveness. It's hard to rebuild a relationship after that. That is probably why many of us are very cautious about bringing up the subject of racism: we stand to lose or damage a relationship, leading to even more isolation than we already experience.

Deb Busman's powerful essay, "When the Killers Are White: White Violence, White Silence," combines personal stories with clear consciousness as she writes of the devastating impact of racism and silence.

Story: It is 1969. I am a teenager, working the graveyard shift at Winchell's Donut Shop because I foolishly think it will be safer than spending more nights on the streets of Los Angeles. The store owner has made a deal that we will provide free donuts and coffee in exchange for high profile police visibility and "protection," and so each night, into the early dawn, the shop fills with shifts of LAPD officers, all male, almost all white, laughing, bragging about their drug busts, racial beatings, and "sexual favors." I am white, young, and invisible except to serve. I am silent, terrified in the presence of such smirking rage and uncensored racial and sexual slurs, such casual hate and brutality. They describe confiscated weed and blowjobs at gunpoint. One cop slams the tables in laughter, telling how he and his partner "fucked us up some beaners and n—s tonight." Two others describe their favorite trick, picking up a young man of color and dropping him off across town in rival gang territory, alone and un-armed. "Black on brown violence, baby. It's a beautiful thing." I do not say a word. My body carries too much personal memory of firsthand police violence from the streets and, though I am protected in this moment by my white skin and crisp, white polyester Winchell's Donut uniform, sweat pours down my back and sides, and I feel the sudden sting of hot piss run down my legs as one of the cops reaches out to hand me a tip.

As a white person in this country, I have been taught to see people of color as the "dangerous" ones. Arabs are "terrorists." Mexicans are "illegal"; immigrants are "stealing our jobs." Young men of color are "gangsters," "thugs." These messages assault me 24/7 via cartoons, music videos, TV news, maga-zines, and U.S. history books. In this supposed "color-blind" society, everything is racialized when it comes to how people of color are portrayed, and criminal-ized, in the media. As James Baldwin reminds us, "Color is not a human or a personal reality; it is a political reality." New Orleans, 2005: AP News carries two separate photos of folks wading through chest-deep waters following Hur-ricane Katrina. In one, a photo of a young, African American man, the caption refers to his "looting a grocery store." In the other, a shot of a young white couple, the caption tells of their "finding bread and soda" from a local store. Who "finds" and who "loots"? Who is criminalized, unlawful? Who is human-ized, even resourceful?

■   ■   ■

Story: Chicago, 2011: CBS news station WBBM covers a story of recent South Side shootings, one sixteen year old killed, two teens injured. The (white) news anchors lead into the story, and then cut to footage at the nighttime crime scene, where a four-year-old African American boy is interviewed. "What are you going to do when you get older?" the reporter asks the child. The boy responds, "I'm gonna have me a gun," and then the story cuts to another bystander and the news anchor's voice-over commentary. The white, male voice frames the "disturbing" story: "That is very scary, indeed." What the boy said next, what was cut from the interview and later discovered in unedited footage, was that he would have a gun when he grew up because he was "going to be the police." But that truth, a young man concerned about the violence in his community, wanting to become a police officer, does not fit the master narrative, and so is left on the cutting room floor. The message is clear: young black men are dangerous, out of control. The "killer is still at large." Four-year-old boys want to get guns and "that is very scary, indeed."

Meanwhile, a whole lot of white people are doing a whole lot of killing. Tucson, Arizona: a white man opens fire at a supermarket, killing six people, including a judge and a nine-year-old girl and wounding thirteen others, including Representative Gabrielle Giffords. A white man in Norway sets off a bomb attack, then drives to an island, dresses as a police officer, and kills sixty-nine people at a political youth camp. Two white boys kill five people and wound eleven others in an Arkansas schoolyard shooting. A white boy opens fire on a student prayer circle in West Paducah, Kentucky, killing three students. In Pearl, Mississippi, a sixteen-year-old white boy kills his mother, and then goes to school and shoots nine students, killing two. Across the country, white militia men gather guns, make bombs, actively arm themselves for violence each and every day, publicly preparing themselves for battle. A white man known as the Unabomber murders and maims several people, sending bombs out through the mail, destroying limbs, faces, lives. A white man bombs the *Alfred P. Murrah Federal Building* in Oklahoma City, killing and wounding hundreds of people. A white man crashes his plane into the IRS building in Austin, Texas, killing three, leaving behind an "anti-government manifesto" asserting that violence "is the only answer." The list is endless, as are the discussions, the public ponderings of "Why?" "How could this happen?" "What went wrong?" Everything from violent video games to Sarah Palin is blamed for the violence. And no one mentions race.

This country has a vast and horrific legacy of white male violent criminals: Dylan Klebold and Eric Harris, Richard Speck, Charles Manson, the two men who were named "the Hillside Strangler", Ted Bundy, Son of Sam, the Boston

Strangler, Jeffery Dahmer, Larry Singleton. Serial killers, mass murderers, rapists, terrorists. White. Men. And no one mentions race.

■ ▧ ▨

Stories: Closer to my home in Monterey, California, a white boy attacks another teenager, breaking his neck, leaving him paralyzed. The newspaper headline reads: "Carmel High Student Hurt Wrestling"; the article tells how the two boys were innocently "rough-housing." Two white young football players from Monterey Peninsula Community College beat up a man outside the local gay bar, bashing his face into a car, kicking him into the gutter, knocking him unconscious. The judge refuses to charge them with a hate crime, buying the defense argument that, "Oh, they were just a couple of healthy young men who had a little too much to drink, out looking for a fight. The victim just happened to get in their way." A white man in his sixties, a former school administrator, murders his wife in their Pebble Beach home and loads her body into his late model sedan. He is arrested later on the shoulder of Highway One in Marina as he straps her body into the driver's seat, fastening the seatbelts, preparing to stage a car accident. Another white man, former Carmel psychologist and college instructor James Nivette, murders his ex-wife, leaves his toddler son wandering the streets, and flees to Paris. A flood of Nivette's former girlfriends, students, and patients comes forth with stories of rape, violence, threats, and coerced sexual encounters. And no one mentions race.

We—white folks, journalists, TV news commentators—do not "talk" race when it is white people doing the violence. After all, these incidents weren't "about" race, were they? Yet, race was foremost in many people's minds when the federal building was bombed in Oklahoma and the crazed search immediately began for an "Arab terrorist." When the killer was found to be white, race was no longer a subject of discussion.

Can you imagine what the news would look like if any or all of the above killings had been done by a black man? A black man bombing the federal building? A black man murdering fourteen women in Montreal? Black men opening fire across the nation, murdering people at post offices, schools, McDonalds, 7-Elevens. A black man murdering a judge and a nine-year-old girl, shooting a congresswoman point blank in the head, Black boys murdering teachers and children at schools and church gatherings. Black boys publicly trained in the use of handguns, rifles, and assault weapons, publicly praised for their high scores in local town shooting competitions. Can you imagine what the police response would be to groups of thousands of armed, angry black militiamen gathering in the towns and woods across the country, publicly declaring war on the U.S. government? Or if black or brown or Arab American men, dressed in Tea Party hats, called for the "lynching" of congressional enemies and said they were ready to "suit up, get my gun, go to Washington, and do what they trained me to do." If that many African American—or Latino, or Native American, or Asian American, or Arab American—men were acting that violent, you can believe this country would be talking about race. And yet, when the killers are white, no one mentions race.

When the killers are white, newscasters report on the "shock" and "confusion" neighbors, friends and people across the country feel at this "outrage," this "unthinkable" act. Every person interviewed (almost always white people) after a white schoolyard/shopping center shooting expresses shock, sorrow, and bewilderment. The perpetrator is seen as a "bad apple," a "deranged individual." Everyone shakes their heads sadly, asking, "Why?" "How could this be?" Yet, I wonder, if black interviewers asked members of nearby communities of color about their reactions to the white schoolboy killers, would we see the same stunned, confused expressions that we see on the pale midwestern faces?

Black people in this country know that white people are "crazy"—dangerous, unpredictable, violent, "not quite right." They live with it every day. It is not news. That "white folks are crazy" is only a secret in white communities; in communities of color, people have known and suffered from, endured and resisted this fact for centuries. How else to explain church bombings and the horrific murders of four young black girls in a Birmingham church? How else to explain a people who gather their entire families in picnic, social celebration, and laughter at the public lynchings of other human beings?

As the media begins to spin their analysis of the violence into larger issues of social concern, questions are asked about gun control, TV violence, video games, and lack of adequate role models. One journalist even goes so far as to blame the Jonesboro schoolyard murders on the women's liberation movement, saying that working mothers and legalized abortion were responsible for these two boys opening fire on their female classmates. More than one feminist pointed out that the killers were boys, the victims mostly girls. But, nowhere in the white-dominated media have I seen mentioned the race of the two murderers. News coverage lapses into the familiar color-blindness we've come to expect in this country when a white person commits a crime—this is not about race, it's about two young "boys," a personal tragedy.

It is a long-standing tradition of white culture and media to racialize acts of violence when they are committed by people of color and deracialize them when they are committed by whites. When a person of color commits a crime, two things happen immediately: the person gets dehumanized/ultra-racialized and their entire race goes on trial. When a white person commits a crime, it is an individual instance, an exception. It's personal, not racial. "He was such a nice young man," white neighbors in housedresses say in TV interviews in Arkansas, Texas, California, Arizona, Colorado, Oklahoma. "We never would have suspected." And you know these same earnest women clutch their purses and lock their doors every time they encounter a young man of color, immediately "suspecting" danger, seeing "race," never seeing "a nice young man."

Racism is never just about white people holding stereotypes about or doing harm to people of color. It is also about an inability, or rather unwillingness, to "see" whiteness. White racism is about being able to choose when, where, and how we see race. It is about having the privilege to decide when race "matters" and when it is irrelevant, not an "issue." Racism is about the institutionalized privilege that allows us the power to name who is dangerous and who seems like "such a nice man." As whites, we are taught to see violence and danger in the bodies and behavior of "other" races. *That* is where the danger lies. Immigrants, blacks, Mexicans. *They* are the criminals. *They* are whom we must fear. We are taught to look "down," to look "away," never to look in the mirror.

Stories: After murdering her two children, Susan Smith, a white woman from South Carolina, tells police that she had been carjacked by a black man who stole her car and kidnapped her sons. Bonnie Sweeton stages an elaborate hoax alleging she and her nine-year-old daughter were kidnapped by two "black men" when, in reality, she had drained her husband's account of $12,000 and taken her kid to Disney World. White Boston salesman Charles Stuart murders his wife and unleashes police to run roughshod over the black community for weeks with his false accusation of an African American perpetrator. In 2010, twenty-eight-year old Bethany Storro made the news with her story of the "African American female" who "threw acid on her face," only to admit a month later that her injuries were self-inflicted.

The racial displacing of danger and violence onto men of color is so extreme for whites that, during the Rodney King trial in L.A., a white jury found four white officers innocent of assault, even though they were caught on video viciously beating and kicking King, a black man, as he lay on the ground. Even though the video clearly showed that over fifty-six baton blows were delivered, along with numerous kicks and stun gun blasts; even though there were twenty-one LAPD officers on the scene at the time; even though King suffered nine skull fractures, a broken cheek bone, a shattered eye socket, and a broken leg; the jury found that it was King, not the white policemen, who was "dangerous." In 2009, Oscar Grant, a twenty-three-year-old African American, was shot in the back and killed by a white BART police officer in Oakland as he lay face down, unarmed, surrounded by police and bystanders with cell phone cameras, capturing everything. Officer Johannes Mehserle would later claim the murder was a "mistake" and that he thought he had grabbed his taser, not his gun. Mehserle served less than two years in prison and was released in June 2011. Even when it was right in front of their faces, "proven" on video, the white jurists still could not "see" white violence.

I can see it. I see it everywhere. And it sickens and frightens me. As a white person raised in this country I have been taught, like everyone else, to see other races as violent, dangerous. I have been taught to fear people of color and that I am supposed to act "surprised" when a white man murders and maims.

I am not surprised. I know white violence intimately, in every cell in my body. I have personally known white violence and I have also witnessed it on a daily basis, sometimes firsthand, sometimes on TV news. Almost every white woman I know has experienced rape, date rape, domestic violence, or sexual abuse at the hands of white boyfriends, white fathers, uncles, brothers. Virtually every white man I know has experienced physical violence at the hands of other white men—fathers, older brothers, coaches, white boys at playgrounds, schools, streets, basic training camps. I think we white people are fooling ourselves when we try to pretend that we don't know how dangerous and violent white people can be. To promote the illusion that it is not white people who are dangerous, that it is people of color who are the ones to look out for, is a lie born out of fear. Fear of our own race; fear of those who hold and wield power in often the most brutal of ways.

To speak out about white violence is to break the rules of white silence. White violence. White silence. Twin siblings of destruction, desperate in their need for one another. Fear of violence keeps us silent. We are afraid. We are afraid the violence will turn on us. This is not an ungrounded fear. Much as a man who, when confronting other men on their sexism, will often be turned upon, ridiculed, attacked, called "pussy" and "faggot," white silence and quiescence is similarly enforced. The comfort and protection of privilege can disappear in an instant when true power and abuse is confronted. That is a terrifying realization.

■   ■   ■

Story: It is the early 1990s. I am a successful business owner and respected member of the Chamber of Commerce in a small, mostly-white California community nicknamed "The Last Hometown." There has been a break-in to my print shop, nothing major, probably just some kids jimmying the back door, stealing cds and petty cash. Still, we are advised to file a police report for insurance purposes. The police station is a block and a half up the street, just past the local market. We've been in business at that location for over a decade, and the police know us well as, each year, we donate the flyers for their statewide officer motorcycle competition. Two officers come to the shop, tip their hats, call me "Ma'am" and proceed to take down the report. It is all going fine until they start to hone in their questions, clearly targeting the brother of one of our employees, an African American press operator, as a key suspect. I politely let them know that they are way off base, that I know the young man well. But this is the town where nonwhite drivers are routinely pulled over for questioning. Once, an award-winning visiting gospel church choir was escorted out of town when they stopped at a McDonald's after giving a sold-out performance at the local middle school, apparently frightening the manager who called the police upon seeing "so many black people all at one time."

At first, I joke with the cops, trying to keep it light. "Think about it," I say. "The kids picked through the cds, but only stole the country western ones." But they push harder. I suggest that, if they are going to focus in on the brothers of employees as suspects, they need to talk to my brother and the brother of my business partner, both of whom are white and who visit the shop frequently. My partner's brother is a diagnosed schizophrenic with a police record, but clearly there is only one "brother" the police are interested in. Our conversation becomes increasingly heated. Suddenly, I feel the flip, sense that I have fallen out of the realm of those "protected and served." No longer am I called "Ma'am." Finally, one cop spits at my feet in disgust, turning away to leave. "Come on," he says to his partner. "I've had enough of these f-ing n-loving queers. We're done here." From "Ma'am" to "n-loving queer" in sixty seconds. Race traitor. And suddenly a "deviant" to boot.

As white people, we are not supposed to talk about white racism, much less white violence. We can talk about "the problems of the minorities," we can participate in Welcoming Diversity workshops, but we cannot question the centrality of whiteness. That must remain fixed, a normalized place into which we can graciously welcome "others" and never have to question ourselves. We don't want to feel what it's like to be on the "outside," to be not only not protected, but actually targeted by the dominant group. Above all, we must not mention the violence that is committed under this sickness called white supremacy. Even if we pretend not to, we carry the racial memory of laughing, picnicking lynch mobs. We carry the images of Oscar Grant, unarmed, face-down, shot in the back; of Amadou Diallo, shot forty-one times reaching for his wallet. Seared into our psyche are pictures of Abu Ghraib torture and abuse, white soldiers Charles Graner and Lynndie England standing grinning and thumbs up over the dog-leashed, naked pile of brown-skinned Iraqi prisoners.

I think that in our hearts we know this painful piece of our nation's truth and that it is out of fear that we act as silent accomplices in the perpetuation of the mythology that names peoples of color as the violent, "dangerous" ones in our society. In our hearts, we know the legacies of white violence we have inherited, especially against people of color. We know who it is that has been truly violent and dangerous in this country, who has enslaved, raped, lynched, and executed African peoples, who has stolen land and committed acts of genocide on Native Americans, who has stolen land and labor from Mexicans. It is a history that must be faced, a history that will not disappear no matter the desperate attempts such as Arizona's recent school banning of books and eradication of ethnic studies programs.

Sometimes, as a white person in this country who does "see" white violence, I feel like I'm in the midst of this big family gathering where there is a totally out-of-control family member, an alcoholic uncle, going around acting lewd, breaking things, hurting people, obviously drunk, while all the other members of the family just keep going about their business, making potato salad, serving punch, flipping burgers on the grill, pretending that nothing is wrong. I feel crazy that no one in my "family" mentions the sickness, even though I know that the neighbors talk about it, that everyone else can see the bruises, the broken windows, the clear evidence.

I see it. I see it, not only in our nation's past, our shared history of genocide, slavery, smallpox-infested blankets, internment camps and public lynchings. I see it today, every day. I see it in the execution of Troy Davis, the death penalty a modern-day form of state-sanctioned lynching. I see it in the shooting of Oscar Grant. I see it in the current literal, rhetorical, and legislative attacks on immigrants. I see it every time a young, blond, white girl's face appears on the news, on the missing children's milk cartons, never a young black girl. I see it in the assault on education, the pipeline to prison, the criminalization of young men of color. I see it in Kansas House Speaker Mike O'Neal's recent e-mail prayer, "Pray for Obama. Psalm 109:8–9," referencing a Bible passage which reads, "Let his days be few; and let another take his office. . . . May his children be fatherless and his wife a widow."

Like alcoholism, white violence is a sickness that will not go away if we just pretend not to see it. Like alcoholism, white violence does harm not just to its overt victims, but also to everyone in the family. I do not believe any person or group can dehumanize another without doing damage to their own humanity.

And, like alcoholism, when truth is denied, the disease of racism and white violence circles back upon itself, flush with the shame, only to lash out with even more vicious projected loathing. Like alcoholism, the first step in healing from white violence is to stop and really look at it sober; to take the blinders off and admit that there is a serious problem.

Following his reception of the Nobel Peace Prize for his work as an opponent of apartheid, South African Archbishop Desmond Tutu is quoted as saying, "Be nice to the whites; they need you to rediscover their humanity." While I don't believe it is the job of people of color to restore our humanity, I do believe Archbishop Tutu is exactly right in his naming of the damage done to white people under systems of racial oppression and injustice. And, yes, it does take tremendous courage, humility, and strong-heartedness to truly face the violence done under white supremacy, the heartbreaking dehumanization of peoples that continues each and every day. But I know that it is possible, and I know that denial, acquiescence, and guilt (silence's equally paralyzing and deadly twin sister) are not our only options.

Learning our history—all of our history, including the histories of oppression, but also the equally silenced narratives of white resistance, alliances, and cross-racial social justice coalitions—is critical, as is the speaking out against injustice. Dr. Martin Luther King Jr. once said, "Our lives begin to end the day we become silent about things that matter," and I would argue that for whites, a first step in reclaiming our full humanity, in beginning rather than ending our lives, is found in the very breaking of silences that bind systems of oppression in place. I believe there is healing in the resistance; healing in the embracing of the old Industrial Workers of the World (IWW) motto, "An injury to one is an injury to us all," healing that comes when we choose to live and act out of our own, full humanity.

7 Separation from Adults (Acquaintances, Friends & Lovers)

*The choice was . . . between wholeness and division in the family of man . . .
between integration and disintegration in our very hearts, between love and
hate—between the highest and the lowest values I knew.*

Sarah-Patton Boyle, 1962

Among the many privileges of adulthood is the ability to choose one's own
friends and lovers. When a system of exclusion interferes with that ability,
adults sometimes experience it as oppression and sometimes as loss. In either case, it is accompanied by grief. The writers in this chapter explore the
ways in which racism has affected their adult relationships.

It is not uncommon for relationships with adult family members
to change as consciousness increases. Sometimes those relationships are
strengthened; sometimes they become estranged. Strong emotions are almost always involved.

Diana shares another memory as she continues to trace the impact of
racism on her life.

Diana writes:

My sister, whose only daughter was fathered out of wedlock by a Mexican
American high school friend, prided herself on bringing up her daughter without
prejudice toward other races. When she and our mother picked up Patie from
her first day of kindergarten, they were surprised to see Patie coming down the

path holding hands with a little black boy. They enjoyed telling the story over and over again. They laughed and thought it was "so cute and sweet," but said that they were "not expecting that!" as though they were not expecting her to go that far.

Eventually, I heard the story in a different way. It was not as funny. I was confused, hurt, and disappointed by the subtle innuendo, and I started to doubt my sister in other ways as well. I thought she had been intent on racial equality, and I was proud of my big sister for that. Now, I no longer trusted her words.

Although having identical racial identification meant that Leon was able to fit in with the professional students in workshops he facilitated, his consciousness of their values and their racism created emotional separation and distressing memories.

Leon writes:

It isn't easy to find words to describe the racism of the teachers in remote communities and on the small islands of Alaska in the late seventies and early eighties. I was traveling to several districts and local schools teaching a workshop on the changing family—a challenge for teachers. Each district seemed to have a superintendent who hired his teachers from the area of South Alaska he was from. Those teachers were there for a few years in order to benefit from room and board, to receive a high salary, and to make a quick buck. Then they would leave these islands and kids. While I was there in the teachers' boarding houses, they made derogatory and racist remarks about the kids and families as if they were "other." I never forgot.

There are times when a history of segregation and de facto segregation engender continued separation, even when there is desire for connection between people who have similar interests and different racial identifications.

Tom writes of leaving a community where everyone lived with sameness and moving to a racially diverse community in which interracial friendships still seemed impossible to achieve.

Tom's story:

In the mid-1970s, business career advancement compelled me to move my family from Maine to a small rural town in Tennessee. My son and daughter were high school age and, for lack of opportunity, had no interaction with people of other races. Portland was nearly 100 percent white at the time. I had gone to school knowing members of three black families. I recall no instances of racism toward these fellow students and athletes. My children grew up in a suburb without a black family in residence. Their minds were blank pages with regard to race.

I had no thought that racism would be a factor affecting our relocation to the South. After all, wasn't this 1975? At first I didn't notice it, but it was there. My initial clue came when we attended a high school football game. My son, a soccer player at home, was recruited to be the specialty kicker. We chose a seat in the empty stands near the 30-yard line to be well positioned to watch him kick extra points and field goals. The seats between the 35-yard lines were roped off and filled. I assumed they were reserved seats. I was correct in my assumption, but for the wrong reason. The seats were filled with white people, some who looked at us curiously. The teams warmed up and still we sat alone. I was clueless, happy to have great seats to watch my son kick. Just as the game was about to begin, hundreds of black people came through the gates and filled the stands from the end zone to the 35-yard line. We sat, two white faces now surrounded by the black fans. More curious looks from the reserved seats followed. We watched the game ignored by our seatmates. No one spoke. Nods were exchanged.

The next home game found us in the same position, alone in the stands until the wave of black fans took their seats around us. Still Jan and I didn't understand the significance of our situation until we heard a small girl's voice behind us say, "Daddy, those white folks are here again!" I turned, located her and said "Yes, and we will see you here at all the home games." My accent coupled with our presence must have given me away because her father said, "You must be Michael's daddy." "I am," I said, and reached out to shake his hand. Other handshakes followed. We then heard good things about our son from all seated around us and talked football until the game began. We were warmly received each week the team played at home. But as we sat alone watching the warm-ups, we still received curious glances from the folks in the midfield stands. I would like to say that we became friends with our seatmates, but that did not happen outside the confines of the football field. Hundreds of years of history and culture in that town precluded any such storybook ending. Michael was a senior that year. We didn't attend football games after he graduated and never saw any of our seatmates again.

One of the ways that immigrant groups attempt to fit in is to align themselves as closely as possible with the dominant group. In the United States, that group was originally English and white. For new arrivals with white skin, the ability to fit in physically has, therefore, always been easier than for immigrants whose skin color is black or brown or yellow, yet they too have been met with prejudice and mistreatment. Sometimes their damaged self-esteem and the desire to be seen as true Americans strengthens empathy and alliance with people of color; sometimes it fosters or strengthens racism.

As Markie shares her understanding of the roots of her father's racism, she offers a powerful example of one of the costs of racism for white people (i.e., the loss of individual ethnic identity as a result of assimilation).

Markie writes:

My father and his siblings emigrated from Norway to the United States when they were young children and continued to be raised speaking Norwegian. When my father's oldest brother, Melford, went to school, he was told he was "stupid," and he flunked the first grade because he only spoke Norwegian. That sent a strong message to the family that the children must speak English. As a result, my father and his siblings spoke and speak little of their native language.

Their language, originally a source of pride, was turned into a source of shame because of others wanting them to assimilate into the U.S. Anglo-Saxon culture. Consequently, my father felt shame about not having a chance to pass the language onto his children, for he believes that led to a loss of much of the culture. I remember growing up with my father making angry statements about immigrants who come over here and do not learn the English language. I used to think that he was simply being prejudiced. However, I have come to realize that his anger around that topic comes from the pain his family experienced from forced assimilation, the shame of not being able to share his native language with his children, and envy of newer families whom he perceives as not having to make the same kind of cultural sacrifice to be citizens. As I pointed that out to him, we both realized that he is most angry with the United States at the time of our family's immigration for not allowing the same kind of cultural pluralism that exists for many families today.

Carol's story also tells of the pain of discrimination based on race and national heritage and of the important and painful lessons learned when she, a teacher, allowed herself to be a student.

This is Carol's story:

As a historian whose research method always includes oral histories, I have had the opportunity and privilege to interview many people of all races, classes, and walks of life. The distance, the care in conversation that people of color often take, the caution of not knowing how this white person would react to something said or done hurts terribly. I want to scream that I am not like that, not like them, not like other racist white people . . . but am I? We all grew up in one of the most race-conscious and racist societies in the world, the United States of America. How can we possibly avoid being affected and infected by racist ideologies that privilege whiteness?

I experienced firsthand the pain of personal racism as a child in California accompanying my Nonna to a bakery in Gilroy, when I realized with shame and horror that the "Dagoes" a tall, nicely dressed, blonde white woman referred to were . . . us. Nonna was dressed as usual in mismatched clothes, did not speak English at all well, and had a tendency to swear in public. This small experience, this little thing, stayed with me forever. One consequence of racism is that one becomes not who we are, but black or white or Asian or Mexican— lumps of categories, outsiders to one another.

Mexicans were not allowed access to public facilities in L.A. in the 1950s. My friend and colleague, who is Mexican American, recounted his parents being turned away from a hospital emergency room because they were Mexican. Their young daughter suffered severe burns and died as a result of lack of medical treatment. As a mother, I find that the horror and pain of that experience is beyond all comprehension, and yet I imagine it and think about how it would be if she were my daughter.

As a scholar doing research on minority-majority communities, I have heard countless stories of demeaning treatment, especially of blacks, who as children were spat upon, abused, tormented because of their race. I know from research and other scholars' work that this abuse extended well beyond the personal to an enormous structural wall of exclusion that left entire populations out of the economy, American social life, and the body politic.

When I am taking oral histories, and in all other interactions, my intention is to look each person deeply in the eye, to see the person I am looking at and to have that person see me. But just when I think I have that connection, it can so easily vanish as a consequence of the legacy of racism in American history and life.

After teaching college- and graduate-level courses on the subject in American history for thirty years, my entire academic career, I thought I knew about race and racism. However in 2006, when I took on the task of researching and writing the history of Seaside, California, a minority-majority city on the Monterey Peninsula, I realized that I didn't know anything at all.

As a white person, I never had to think about race unless I chose to, much less confront the deep and ugly reality of being a person of color in America. As I experienced the consequences of my intellectual alignment with the communities of color in Seaside, I suddenly felt the brunt of white privilege—and white anger when that privilege was called into question. The strong reaction on the part of so many whites was wholly unexpected, painful, and crazy-making. It created a feeling of anger and frustration within me that I found overwhelming most of the time. It also made me determined to persevere, to complete the project, to publish a book.

I had little idea of life in Seaside. My first encounter with its history began with the all-white Historical Commission. Although I had been approved by the city manager of the Seaside City Council to construct a narrative history of the city, the members of the Historical Commission were openly resistant. Most of them were women, but both the women and the men became hostile when I asked questions about the racial composition of the city. Their faces and responses mostly reflected fear. They closed down. They refused to talk with me or to give me access to sources. The city manager, Ray Corpuz, had to intervene, wrest control of source materials, and forcibly allow access to what was haphazardly collected in a mold-filled house on LaSalle Street. I was stunned by what I considered to be an odd and misguided protectionism (of what? I wondered at the time) but also alerted that questions of race, racism, and racial interactions were likely going to be an important part of Seaside's story. I soon realized that the ladies at the Historical Commission were protecting a white narrative, a story of Seaside frozen in the nineteenth century when its residents were white and middle class. That moment lasted barely a decade and had little to do with Seaside's eventual development as one of the most important sites for civil rights activism in the state of California or its connection to Fort Ord, one of the largest and most important military training bases on the West Coast.

The hostility got worse. As I organized events, created drafts of the history to share with the community, and wrote articles in local media about Seaside, I found myself facing a small but aggressively vocal and mostly white antagonism that I found both bewildering and painful. A former judge became red-faced, accusing me of "playing the race card" and insisted that I drive around Seaside with him so that he could point out the bars and clubs frequented by black people to prove how seedy and notorious Seaside was when African Americans were considered to be numerically ascendant. Several white residents expressed their resentment loudly when the city hosted an exhibit sponsored by our project celebrating its communities of color, as though this would somehow lessen the value of whites in the community. As I faced these residents, I thought to myself that they would be the first ones to dismiss any objections a person of color might have over a white-dominated historical exhibit as "overly sensitive" or "silly."

That work is completed, the book is now available, and I am a changed person. I learned to feel and appreciate the real evil and power of racism, usually unacknowledged as such, as it denigrates, denies personhood, and tries to render even the most critical historical actors invisible. Most importantly, I came to understand in my heart how racism is held onto and defended at all costs. That will pain me always.

Within a few years of first awakening to the devastating relationship between race and class, Caroline's deep friendship with an African American man was challenged by his family's feelings about their racial difference. Intense emotion and a sense of powerlessness were created by both experiences.

Caroline's story:

I moved to Haiti in 1984. After graduating from college and working for a public health department, some friends and I decided to work abroad, doing international health education. We found a small not-for-profit organization in Haiti that needed us and, with much excitement, headed off to make the world a better place!

I had never seen such poverty or such enormous disparity between the rich and the poor. Issues of race and class collided right smack into each other as I attempted to make sense of what I was seeing and experiencing. What I had taken for granted as a small child growing up in a segregated part of the United States was now under enormous scrutiny as my developing and awakening consciousness struggled to understand what was going on in Haiti and what part I played in all of it.

Naively, I had assumed that we would be living in the same rural community in which we were providing health care. Not so. We lived in one of the largest houses in town, had several Haitian people working for us, and were considered wealthy white ex-patriots. (I even had my underwear ironed the entire time I lived there, no matter how many times I said it was not necessary!) Marie, the woman who cooked and cleaned for us, was paid $12 a week, the highest salary of all her peers.

Haiti was a crash course in how the world actually worked. While working with a Haitian doctor, I met a young woman with HIV. In the entire country of Haiti, there were only six hospital beds for people with AIDS. Haitians had also been initially considered a risk group, as if being Haitian, rather than the lack of access to necessary resources, was the reason people were infected with HIV. As I recall this story, I still find myself angry and sad at the dehumanization caused by the intersection of racism and classism. I can still feel the powerlessness of not being able to change the situation.

When I was twenty-six, I moved from Haiti to New York. I went to New York to go back to graduate school and I took a job on a start-up project, working with homeless people who had substance abuse or mental health problems. The city department of mental health funded my agency, and we had site visits from the project manager assigned to our organization. His name was Vince, he was African American, and we liked each other immediately. After I left the organization we stayed connected, and we remain good friends today. During my six years in New York, Vince and I would hang out together. Vince came to my birthday parties, met my friends, and attended my wedding, but never once did I get invited to his house. Never once did I meet his family, all of whom lived in New York. I was married and living in California before I was included in anything that took me into Vince's personal life.

In 1993, on one of my trips to New York, Vince invited me to his brother's art opening. I was excited to be included and looked forward to attending. Vince was not there when I arrived, so I went into the gallery to look around and enjoy the exhibit. I noticed that I was one of the only white people in the room. Having lived in Haiti, I had experienced this before. However, I remember feeling uncomfortable and anxious and embarrassed about my feelings. I wished Vince were there. When Vince did arrive, he introduced me to his mother. She was cordial, but not welcoming. Several of Vince's friends were also cold and distant, as if they disapproved of my being there. I remember realizing that this was not about me, that this was about what I represented, that this was one of the horrible costs of racism. I remember realizing, again, how much white people (ME!) had to learn about the devastating effects of racism. It had never occurred to me that I would not be welcomed in Vince's world. I was accustomed to being treated warmly and with interest. I was surprised that I could meet such indifference, even hostility, from people who were meeting me for the first time. Even with the insight I had, the sadness was overwhelming. Vince could see what was going on and kept apologizing. I told him that this was nothing he had caused. I was being offered another lesson, another personal teaching on race relations in the United States. While I am grateful for being open to the learning, the sadness is still with me every time I think about that experience.

Intimate love relationships that cross lines of racial identification are, perhaps, the most serious threat to a system of institutionalized racism and racist conditioning. Living in a society that is permeated with racism while being without the support of family and friends makes such relationships very difficult to maintain. The Supreme Court decision of 1967 in *Loving v. Virginia* legalized interracial marriages throughout the United States. Although attitudes toward interracial relationships have become significantly more positive during the past generation, many people continue to grieve the impact of the history of U.S. apartheid.

Recalling memories that stretch across five decades, the following writers share challenges they faced and grief they experienced as they remember their loves.

This is Judy's story:

Doris Day sang it so sweetly: "Once I had a secret love, who lived so deep inside of me." That song represented my life for my entire teenage years. It was the mid-fifties when, looking back, life in general seemed so easy. But my father was suffering from a congenital heart defect, and he was getting weaker day after day with an illness that lasted for seven years. While the severity of his sickness was mostly kept from my sister and me, we knew things were not right, and still we did what we needed to move ahead.

I was one of the "popular" girls with lots of friends and a happy-go-lucky personality. While a very good student, I rarely studied hard and was a good example of the eternal optimist. In the evenings, after schoolwork was done, I jabbered on the phone with my girlfriends and listened to the then-new rhythm and blues music. Despite Dad's illness, my life was good.

In our community, junior high was a four-year cycle. We started in seventh grade and graduated after tenth. Then there were two years of high school. We were fortunate to attend a school that was almost equally racially mixed. At McKinley Junior High the student population was one-quarter Asian, one-quarter Hispanic, one-quarter black, and one-quarter Caucasian. While our social connections were usually within our own ethnic group, there was friendly banter with everyone. It was in 1954, while I was going steady with another boy, that I met my first true love, Richard Scott. I didn't mean to fall for him; it just happened, and it hit me so hard that the feelings could not be denied. Here was a guy who had everything. He was the epitome of strength, good looking, elected president of the school, and a star athlete in every sport, with an incredibly calm, all-around friendly demeanor. He was just one great person. Everyone liked him; everyone looked up to him. Like Raymond Edwards, the bass singer with the Silhouettes singing "Get a Job," his voice was deep and resonant. When he spoke in front of the student body everyone was quiet and in awe. When he smiled and laughed he filled the room with amazing positive energy.

Starting in eighth grade, boys were calling, and it was the "thing" to go steady, which I did a couple of times before encountering Richard. The first time I saw him was in band class. He played the tuba, the perfect instrument for a guy whose voice was as low as the lower notes on his musical sheet. My two girlfriends and I chose to play clarinets, and we had fun as we learned how to read the notes and play the songs.

At first Richard was just another guy in the class. I really hardly noticed him. But one day, out on the yard, some of the guys were teasing some of the girls. I heard Richard's beautiful voice, and I stood there, almost mesmerized, watching this Adonis-like creature walk across the blacktop. That was it! I came home and began writing in my diary. The next week, I broke up with my boy-friend, Steve, as I no longer had any feelings for him whatsoever.

Although the whole thing confused Steve, I couldn't tell him that I had fallen hard for a black guy. In 1954 it just was not the acceptable or proper thing to do for a "nice" girl like me. I also had to keep the secret from my dad. He was extremely disturbed by my sister's relationship with a Mexican boyfriend, so I knew how prejudiced he was. Although Richard's family was very welcoming of me, I had no support for being public with our relationship, other than having two friends who helped us find ways of getting together. It had to be kept secret because of racism. However, the day that it began was the start of an adventure that left an indelible mark on my life.

In 1956 my dad died; my mom, my sister, and I moved shortly afterward; and I had to give away my dog. It was a very difficult time, and my relationship with Richard felt like the source of my life force, giving me more resilience and internal strength than any other motivating factor. My love for him was so big that I couldn't give it up. We were together for four more years and then separated, in part because he was so protective of my mom's feelings. She was a young widow and had so much to deal with.

Decades later, when we met for lunch as friends, I was so proud of being in his presence in public. To this day, I continue to have sound, good, exciting, loving memories of an unequaled love, an unfulfilled, yet still fulfilling, relationship. I loved him so deeply, and I've told many friends about him. It is a real tragedy that in the 1950s and 1960s such a relationship was not socially acceptable.

Gayle writes:

As an eighteen year old at San Jose State in 1966, I was active in a project called Operation Share, in which a group of us starry-eyed freshmen served as tutors to at-risk elementary students. It opened up my love of young children and was a catalyst for thirty-three years in a social work career. I was paired up with another student, and we did home visits together. We became great friends. Later, we became a couple. That relationship lasted for eight years.

I am about as white as you can get; Frank is African American. I was initially naive beyond imagination and really didn't pay much attention to the reactions of friends, neither his nor mine. I was simply swept up in a new relationship that seemed so right. Temperaments clicked, values shared, and love was in the air. There was all of that. He was on a full-ride football scholarship, and he was an outstanding student as well as an activist. I was so proud that he supported John Carlos and Tommie Smith in their Black Power salute at the Mexico Olympic Games in 1968, took a leadership role on campus with the Black Athletes Association that sponsored the boycott of the Brigham Young University football game following their refusal to admit black students, and that he was articulate and active in political events. I was little prepared for the onslaught of not-so-subtle racist comments from roommates, intense looks from strangers, being banished to the back table of a restaurant, getting drilled with questions by an Oakland cop at a traffic stop, receiving sexually explicit notes on my car windshield, and being denied lodging while on the road.

Having grown up in a cocoon, with all the right words at home and in church about how "God created all his children to love one another," I was saddened and disappointed beyond words at my own parents' reaction. Frank was never welcomed with more than tepid enthusiasm.

On the other hand, we spent many holidays at his family home, where both his mother and father embraced me, hugged me up and down, knew my dreams, and supported my college goals as well as my love of their only son. We had late-into-the-night discussions about what we might face as a couple, and they gently guided me to know a world far bigger than anything I'd ever experienced. Franky's mom taught me to cook, I became active in their church, and though I couldn't sing a lick, I learned all the powerful music that was celebrated in the choir.

Franky's sisters were another story. They were two years older than I, and "icy" would be an understatement as to how I was received. They did not want a white girl snatching up their brother, and they made it plain for all to see. My heart was pierced by the coldness; I couldn't figure out what I had done to bring this on. One day they simply told me that, no matter what their mother thought, I could never be part of their family.

Those years were tumultuous and energizing politically, but also polarizing. People literally became quite black and white in their thinking about militant racial views. I listened, I learned, and I waited for the division in Frank's family to settle, thinking that, in due time, it would. While we were good as a couple, the pressure and disruption our relationship caused between his sisters and parents and between him and the sisters he loved was painful and ongoing. They were tightly knit in many ways, and his commitment to me was defined as disloyal and a betrayal. In the end, we went separate ways for many reasons, and the reaction of his sisters was one of them.

Ten years ago, at the ripe old age of fifty-two, I got a letter from one of Frank's sisters telling me "Now as a grown woman I feel ashamed and want to make amends for how you were treated . . . at the time you seemed very much to represent something that I only knew to hate . . . a white girl who had everything. That is not how I was raised, nor is it how I raised my sons."

I have wondered many times how life would have been had we stayed together. We laughed at the same things, had similar goals for careers, were passionate about human rights, and loved a widely diverse group of friends. He has had a rich, good life, is married to a wonderful lady, raised two glorious daughters, both of whom are much like him in accomplishment. One even played soccer at the Olympic Games in Australia. He writes every once in a while and sends pictures, as I do in return. I wouldn't trade my husband and family for anything, but I still think about this first big love and how the racial divide had a part in bringing it to an end.

Leatha shares:

I am white and I first dated, then lived with, and then married a black man. I tell it to you that way because it took us seven years to marry. By that time we had a four-year-old daughter. Then, we had a second daughter. Our marriage lasted ten years. We lingered separated another five years before we divorced.

I was raised in Wyoming by parents who grew up on dirt farms. They were World War II vets, college educated, liberal, and very political people. There were seven children in my family.

My ex-husband is the son of a Baptist minister and a registered nurse who were both raised in the Columbus, Georgia, and Phenix City, Alabama, areas. Other families from that part of the country wrote to them about opportunities in Paso Robles, California, and in the early sixties they made that move, bringing their five children with them. After I had been married for many years, my father-in-law told me that they were looking for a better life and running from "the danger that the Civil Rights movement stirred up." Eventually, there were seven children in that family.

My ex-husband's parents were careful around white people and they were uncomfortable with me, but they were always kind.

In 1979, the year in which my ex-husband and I met, most black women seemed to me to be very hostile to white women dating black men. This included my ex-husband's sisters. Though they were courteous to me, they advised him strongly against marrying "a white woman" and questioned me about my motives. It is also true, however, that our closest friends as a couple were either black or interracial couples, and my ex-husband's brothers dated my white friends.

Every year, in order to make a little extra cash, my father-in-law parked cars in his yard across from the fairgrounds during the week of the California Mid State Fair. There was fierce competition among the mostly black or Hispanic families who lived near the fairgrounds and who had parking spaces to sell for the week when the fair blew in. Every family member was pressed into service flagging drivers in. Out-of-town family came to help and to enjoy the fair. They sat on the porches visiting with each other and greeting all their friends crossing the street to enter the fair gates. It was a party atmosphere, especially since you could hear all the music leaking out from the various stages inside. It was also an opportunity for a job in one of the concessions or booths inside. And there was money to be had working security—standing guard over the livestock and exhibits.

The house was crowded, the water cooler was on high, and its air was pushing the oppressive late August heat around. Kids and grown-ups gathered on the porch as the day cooled into evening, dangling their legs off the edge. It was fun! In groups, we would wade with the crowds across the street and come back hot and exhausted, the kids sticky and stuffed with fair food and dizzy from the carnival rides. The whole family loved the fair.

One year when my oldest daughter was three, my father-in-law-to-be took my not-yet-husband aside and asked him to request that I not sit on the porch with my daughter and the rest of the family. He thought that seeing an obviously white member of the family with a not easily explained child might keep his mostly white clientele from choosing his yard for their parking places. By then, he was retired as a minister, but I think that, in addition to the racial issue, he was embarrassed about our marital status. I was devastated and embarrassed, and we went home. In my cheerful and naive optimism, I was unable to see things from his perspective. Although I knew that he had reservations about me, he had always treated his grandchild with love, and it had not occurred to me that his reservations would extend to her. We made him so uncomfortable.

When I think about that experience now, my main feeling is that of sadness for my long-dead father-in-law. I loved him, and I know he loved me, too. I also know that he loved his granddaughter. On that occasion, I believe that deeply entrenched anxieties related to childhood lessons about how to behave around white people got the upper hand. No matter what turmoil there was inside, the surface needed to be smooth. Private life and public life were completely separate. Sitting on the porch for the whole town to see was "letting others see our business." Dangerous, maybe. Uncomfortable at the very least.

Anything that I have to say on the topic of ways in which racism hurts me seems trifling in comparison to my father-in-law's experiences or to those of my sisters-in-law. Fear and sadness and feelings of betrayal also often seem to cloud the issue. However, the evil twisty snake that is racism is wound around my story, too, and is a hurtful reality of life for all of us.

8 Resistance and Freedom

The more contact we have with people of color and with images and information about them, the more we are motivated and equipped to challenge racism. . . . This awareness can guide our action and enrich our lives.

Paul Kivil, 1993

The long, noble struggle for civil rights . . . was a struggle to free white people, too.

President Bill Clinton, 1997

The only thing necessary for the triumph of evil is for good men to do nothing.

Edmund Burke, 1700s

Throughout our country's history, there have been white Americans who fought for racial equality with courage and conviction. They have all taken risks, sometimes with their lives, recognizing that the fight for racial equality is a fight to free us all. Writers in this chapter speak of their experiences resisting racist conditioning and share ways in which they have gained emotional freedom. They offer hope as well as concrete suggestions for creating a more compassionate and just world.

Although stories of adult resistance to a racist society tend to be more frequently told, it is not uncommon for resistance to begin in childhood.

In 1960, six years after the Supreme Court made a landmark decision to desegregate public schools, New Orleans city schools were forced to comply. Two elementary schools (William J. Frantz and McDonough No. 19) were chosen to be the first to have both white and black students. The vast majority of angry and fearful white parents vehemently protested the court order and boycotted the schools, many of them sending their children to a newly created all-white school located in a converted industrial building.

On the first day of the schools' integration one little black girl, Ruby Bridges, and two little white girls were the only children in attendance at Frantz. In order to assure their safety from the mostly female mob that had gathered in protest, the three six-year-olds were escorted to school by U.S. Deputy Marshalls. They were given separate teachers and placed in three separate classrooms.

Yolanda Gabrielle was one of the two white pupils. The other was Pam Foreman. As a consequence of their decision to send Yolanda to school, her family received threats, her mother was taunted with derogatory labels, their home was stoned, and her father, a city water meter reader, lost his job. Unable to support the family of six children and fearing for their safety, he moved them all to Rhode Island, his home state and a place with job opportunities. Yolanda continues to live in Rhode Island, where she is a psychotherapist.

Interview with Yolanda:

Ann: I have read that enrolling you in Frantz Elementary School was primarily your mother's decision, as your dad was concerned about the safety of his job. What are your thoughts and feelings about that difficult decision when you think about her attitudes being controversial ones during that time and in that place?

Yolanda: I have always been proud of my mother for making this decision. She is an example of a person of modest means, living a simple life, who had the courage to do what her higher consciousness told her to do. My mother was, and is, a good woman who strove to do the right thing. She spoke about spiritual matters, compassion for others, while I was still too young to really understand or have such concerns. The difficult decision she made in New Orleans runs true to her character. Although she did not go to college, she was an avid reader, and almost all of the readings were theosophical. When she and my father made the decision, she did speak to me about it. I only remember trusting her logic, trusting that we were doing something "good." Things are simple at that age—another little girl, Ruby Bridges, wanted to go to school and some people were trying to stop that because they did not like the color of her skin—that's not fair. My mom, when confronted with a choice, did not let fear make that decision. She believed in equal rights and did not believe in segregation. Being an immigrant (she came to the United States from Costa Rica at age six), she was sensitive to this issue. I don't think she quite knew how big a decision it would turn out to be.

Ann: What are your thoughts and feelings about your dad following her lead? That was unusual in the white community in 1960.

Yolanda: This speaks both to the nature of their marriage and the nature of my father. Like most men from that era, his decisions were held in higher regard, but he knew when my mother felt strongly about something. She was the moral compass in our family. Also, it was his personality to not want a mob to make his decisions for him.

Ann: How long did you attend that school before your family left for Rhode Island?

Yolanda: I want to say a few months. It is important to note that my parents had moved to Rhode Island, where my father had grown up, one other time before. It had often been discussed. When my father lost his job, the subject obviously came up again. Also, the state police were no longer giving us rides and other help was not consistent. One of my clearest memories of that time is walking alone with my mother through a mob of violent women. I guess I started to have nightmares around that time, although I have no memories of that. My mother became comfortable with the idea of leaving when more and more white parents were bringing their children back to school and there was no longer a possibility of boycotting the school.

Ann: What has the impact of that childhood experience had on your life in general?

Yolanda: Not sure, but if I had to guess, I would say that I have never been a follower. I saw what mob thinking and fear does to people. If parents teach by example, well then this was a big one. I learned how important it was to tap into the source that helps one grow and expand, helps one speak your truth. Obviously, as a therapist, and a teacher before that, I want to encourage others to reach their full potential.

Ann: Have you had any adult relationship with Pam Foreman or Ruby Bridges?

Yolanda: No, I haven't. Unfortunately, and ironically, they kept us separated while at the school. We must have all felt pretty alone . . . I know I did. Moving to Rhode Island soon after, I focused on other six-year-old adjustments.

Ann: Are there people of color in your life now?

Yolanda: I think that the percentage of people of color in Rhode Island is getting larger. When I worked at a hospital in Providence for many years in their Women's Behavioral Health Department (perinatal mood disorders), women of color were at least a third of the population. One of my closest friends is a person of color. However, it is within my own family that I get to experience the most diversity. We try and have the whole family get together at least once a year for my mother's birthday—I have *many* nieces/nephews and great-nieces/nephews. We cover the spectrum of Latino, African American, Native American, Korean, and Caucasian.

Ann: Do you have any thoughts about racism creating mental health issues for members of the dominant group?

Yolanda: I imagine this depends on how severe and consistent the experience. If you are in a relationship with a person of color and ostracized by family and community, the isolation could cause mental health problems . . . or if you are a biracial child and unable to develop an identity that is accepted by family or community. We seem to live in a world where one has to pick a side—not easy on a child.

And then there are the issues for the child who is brought up in a racist family or community, taught to hate from an early age. When I look and listen to skinheads, for example, they certainly look and act like something has gotten so twisted up for them. Any ongoing situation that causes splitting, anger, isolation, loneliness, lack or loss of identity, loss of family and support, etc., can cause mental health issues, and racism certainly can do any or all of these.

Ann: Thanks again for your willingness to contribute to this effort.

There are lots of ways to resist social conditioning. Some forms of resistance are direct, clear, and powerful. Sometimes they are deeply personal.

Brenda F. writes of her experiences as a child after her parents left New Jersey and moved to Georgia. The intersection of racism, classism, and anti-Semitism is woven throughout her decision to find a community in which to belong.

This is Brenda F.'s story:

As a girl growing up in the New Jersey mountains in the 1940s, I had little exposure to the complexities of race and its problems. The only recollection I have is of my father's comments about an old movie I was watching on our twelve-inch television screen. It portrayed a happy-go-lucky fellow tap dancing and repeatedly saying, "Yes, sah, yes, sah." My father commented that "not all colored people" acted the way the movies portrayed them.

When my father told the family we were moving to Georgia because it was a great business opportunity for him, I was chilled: Wasn't Georgia in the heart of the ignorant South, the South that had condoned slavery? My parents reassured me that things were different now and there was nothing to fear from the Southerners. They were, after all, just like the folks who lived a few miles away on the other side of our mountain.

So, we loaded up our home-made trailer with all our furniture and drove south. My dad had built the trailer to haul lumber and building equipment to our beautiful woods, where we had built our tiny dream house. I remember looking longingly out the window of the car as we drove away. From time to time I revisit those tranquil woods in my mind. Part of my soul will always be there.

The first day I went to school in a suburb of Atlanta called Chamblee, I was bowled over by the inattention to the teachers and the total disregard for learning by the students. I was the only student in the class paying attention to the teacher. There were no "colored" students in the entire school . . . so much for public education in Atlanta.

My worried parents found the only alternative schooling available for me at a private girls' school in a beautiful old plantation setting called Washington Seminary. My first day of school was a nightmare! While no one treated me outwardly with disdain, as I was being introduced to the class I could hear the whisper of "Yankee." Throughout that first week I constantly heard the word in hushed tones when I approached. Again, there were no "colored" girls in the school . . . or "colored" teachers.

Some days I rode the city bus to school along Peachtree Street. One morning a lovely young "colored" woman walked down the aisle of the bus. I quickly pulled my topper against me and squeezed over to the window. I smiled at her invitingly, but she looked down and joined her tired friends behind me. The "colored" people did not want to sit with me either. Later I questioned my mother. She explained that the "colored" people had to sit in the back. "That's the law here, Brenda."

I had been slammed into the hateful South I knew was lurking right below the surface, and I was mad now, as well as scared. Never accepted by the polished girls in school who were, at age thirteen, already wearing high heels and pinned to fraternity boys from Georgia Tech, I felt like an out-of-step country bumpkin.

At parties given by the girls' families in their homes, I was invited only if the entire class was as well. There, the only friendly people were the "colored" help. The butler, who spent some time chatting with me, was given the "evil eye" by my classmate's mother. Living and learning, I had a revelation: I was not supposed to speak to the help directly. If I needed something I was to ask the hostess, because that was the purpose of the help: to help, not make conversation.

I felt lonely.

Unlike most of our neighbors, my family during these years never employed any domestic help. As a teenager my mother had been a Mennonite maid in a wealthy home in Winnipeg, Canada, and falsely accused of stealing. We grew up with the idea of being able to clean our own home.

By the time I attended Emory University in Atlanta, I had become quite vocal against the segregation that existed there. There were no "Negro" students and only 15 percent of the students admitted could be Jewish.

While at Emory, I spoke up regularly at sorority meetings in favor of admitting the Jewish sorority to the large house shared by all the other sororities. I was told, "We cannot have them here, because they eat different food." I continued to balk at this absurd reasoning and was eventually asked to repeat my pledge year. I dropped out of the sorority.

One afternoon, while walking on campus, I noticed a very dark, almost coal black, young man strolling congenially with several students. Later, I asked him if he were a student. "Yes," he replied, "in the medical school." I thought that the ban against segregation had been lifted and I started talking with pride about Emory. However, after a few days of celebrating I learned that this student was not considered "colored" by the admissions office "as he came from the Middle East, not the United States or Africa."

Furious, I decided to leave Atlanta and go to New York, to New York University. I could not take this absurd hypocrisy that permeated the South. All my vocalizing and soapbox lectures at Emory had gotten me nowhere.

I also left because I wanted to pursue Judaism. While at Emory, a Methodist university, I was required to attend ten religious lectures presented by leaders from ten different religions. The only speaker who influenced me was Rabbi Rothschild, a reformed Jew, who explained that, as such, he was allowed to question the existence of God. As an agnostic, I so wished for religion for myself and my future family, believing at the time that religion could transcend bigotry and hatred.

At NYU, I met my husband, converted to Judaism, and attended what was probably one of the first African history classes given in a non-black university in this country. To our joy, there were both black and white students in the class. My husband wrote an amazing paper on the history of apartheid while in that class. Yes, I had found my soulmate, and we were fighting the good fight. We were going to raise our children to be not color-blind, but color-celebrators.

Ironically, just a few years after I left Emory, my sister and brother became very active in the civil rights movement in Atlanta. My sister, a staunch fighter and a friend to Martin Luther King Sr., attended many Sunday evening prayer meetings at his home to plan the movement at the local universities. Just four years after I left the South, there was an organized avenue open to her as a college student at Emory to express the need for change and actually cause it to happen. I often speak of her great work and sacrifice with pride.

After years in the Northeast, my husband and I, along with our two elementary-aged children, relocated to California, but the rest of my family remained in the South. My family continues to appreciate the great strides made to improve racial inequalities. Much has changed for the better, but I realize how very much more needs to be accomplished in the South and throughout the country. We have associates in California of our age who still foster racism and bigotry against blacks, Jews, Hispanics, and Muslims.

When asked to write how racism has affected my relationships with people of color while growing up, I thought of the friendships and relationships with other girls and women I had missed and the isolation I had experienced for my beliefs and background. Not until I attended New York University was I successful in having a black friend.

Looking back, though, I realize that the stereotypes I formed against the white Southern girls had certainly been a detriment to my caring for them as friends. I was so worried about their opinions of me that I really did not give them a chance to get to know me. Stereotypes never work, do they?

Alisa's precociousness, Jewish identity, and childhood memory of her African American housekeeper come together in this story about understanding racism before she knew the word. This powerful experience contributed to both her lifelong commitment to fight for social justice and her desire to do so through her music.

Alisa shares:

My memories of Pat, our African American housekeeper, are some of the most vivid from my childhood. As the oldest child of four, I sensed at a young age that my beautiful young mother was not physically or emotionally capable of caring for us on her own. She was only twenty-six when her fourth baby was born. Although Pat was more a disciplinarian than my mother, a task my mother was all too happy to hand over, we felt safe and secure under her watch. When there were arguments among us, she always listened, and verdicts were always just. When my parents went on vacation, Pat cared for us as if we were her children, despite having four children of her own. We felt like we belonged to her and could tell her anything. And yet, when I was about seven years old, I tested that relationship.

We all had our various chores and, being compliant about most things, I always did what I was told. Pat, a large and strong woman, not meant to be crossed, was very strict about handing out orders. After lunch one summer day, I wanted to go out and play. Pat said, "Not until you and your sister do the dishes." I knew it was my chore and my turn, but a wonderful new feeling of defiance surfaced in my small frame, and I replied as plain and calm as day, "Why don't you do the dishes? You're the housekeeper." It was a strange experience because I knew, while I was uttering the words, that it was wrong and wicked, and consequences would be dire. Pat bent over so that her face was in mine. Taking me firmly by the shoulders in her big hands, she began shaking me, and in a deep, loud, and angry voice said, "Don't you ever, ever order me around again, ever!" Knowing that I deserved to be berated and punished, I stood there in silence and soaked in every spit-sprayed word. Pat was so angry that she was salivating. I don't remember being terrified, even though I had never before seen her that angry. I knew she wouldn't hurt me and I knew I deserved everything I had coming to me. I may have been surprised that it didn't last longer. I remember hoping that she wouldn't hate me.

Just before this incident, Pat had been eating a tomato as though it were an apple. I was intrigued because I had never seen that before. I still remember the metallic smell of that red tomato on her warm, angry breath.

I was a victim of anti-Semitism as a child and I knew that, because we were both minorities, we had something in common. I had learned from my parents and my Sunday school teachers that I was to always treat everyone equally. I became cognizant of the unfairness of the world without having been directly told about it. It was on the news and in conversations around me, in the way some of my friends' mothers or relatives would speak to their housekeepers. Still, I must have wanted to challenge or act out what I was experiencing around me. Even back then, I knew I had committed a travesty and understood the weight of my remark and its impact on Pat.

As I write this, I realize that I received exactly the reaction something in me had hoped for. I *wanted* Pat to be mad at me as I tested what I sensed were injustices in friends' homes and even with my beloved grandparents. I knew that my grandparents were wrong, and I grew furious with them if they even muttered a prejudice or something uncomplimentary about black people. I don't think I knew the words "prejudice" or "racism" until my special eighth grade English class, but I was aware that they existed. And I knew immediately after the words had come out of my mouth and I had experienced the depth of Pat's anger that I was testing that "ism." Pat was very proud and she modeled that pride for me, but I sensed, even then at such a young age, that hers was hard-earned. Her reaction to my "order" reinforced in me all I knew that was wrong, and this valuable lesson has stayed with me all my life.

I had only hoped that Pat wouldn't hate me after that, and she didn't; she continued to nurture me and discipline me like her own. I knew that her treatment of me was going to make me better and smarter.

I believe that the opportunity to play out prejudice and oppression in my own way as a young child and to receive Pat's authentic response oriented me on a path of social justice. It was *exactly* the reaction I wanted from Pat, though perhaps not consciously, and I was relieved to get it from her! I don't know if my words can do justice to this feeling I have. I am very grateful to her. Pat opened my eyes and ears even more and affirmed the sense of injustice I had felt at times among people I loved who were treating people of color and social class differently than me. I was confused and troubled by that. Everything I knew that was right and just inside was solidified at that time by Pat's reaction to my comments. I had even more respect for her than before. Pat cleared it up in one fell swoop and heightened the humanity in my young self, giving me a path to become more conscious, sensitive, and alert in the world as I grew up.

I even learned to like tomatoes, although it wasn't until I was fourteen years old and working on a kibbutz in Israel that I saw anyone else take a tomato from the field and bite into it like the fruit that it is.

Long after Pat left, I discovered my parents' collection of the Newport Folk Festival recordings that they received from being members of the Book of the Month Club. I took their collection into my bedroom where I played and replayed the songs over and over, especially Odetta singing "Midnight Special" and "Hold On" which I learned to sing and play on guitar. Odetta's voice was strong, beautiful, and powerful; it came from her belly. Her power reminded me of Pat, and I began to associate that with other African American women. I fell in love with Odetta's voice and began to emulate her as I learned to discover my own voice. I wanted to feel the power of singing like that in my body. Odetta sang as though her singing would make a difference in the world. She profoundly influenced my desire to be a folk-singer.

As he shares childhood memories, Peter speaks of the lessons he learned, of affection for his African American friends, and of respect for his mother's integrity. As was true for Yolanda, Peter's experience offers an example of the maltreatment that is frequently given to racial allies. Such maltreatment is always aimed at keeping the system of racism in place.

This is Peter's story:

My name is Peter. I am a fifty-four-year-old white man. I grew up in the small coastal town of Pacific Grove on the Monterey Peninsula located in what is referred to as central California. My first memory of meeting black children was in 1963 when I enrolled in the public school system. It was a time when African Americans were referred to as "Negro" or "colored." I was five years old.

Many of the kids I met at this time I still know to this day. We always have a great embrace—the women and the men. There seems to be a timeless bond between us, and I cherish it. As I write this, I am transported back to that time and I can see the faces clearly: Edward Issac, Tommy Campbell, Dirrick Williams, Cynthia Dorsey, Jeanetta Files, Stephanie Lewis. I had many friends when I was young, but the one that stands out the most was a young boy named William

Leslie Whyte. (How ironic a last name!) He lived at 410 Sinex Avenue in Pacific Grove. The house has since been renovated.

William was a couple of years older than me and lived with his pretty sister Beverly, older brother James, and younger brothers Greg and John. I'm sad to say that he passed away in February 1996 at the age of forty. He and Greg both died from an illness passed on to them from their father. There isn't a day that goes by that I don't think about him.

I met William across the street from where I lived in 1964. We had a common interest in music and cars, and, when we were a little older, we would walk downtown to Sprouse-Reitz, a now defunct five-and-dime store, to look at car model kits. Now, mind you, going in there by myself as a nine year old, I never had an "escort" following me to any part of the store. But when I came in with a young black boy, the change was dramatic! The employees would not be shy about that. A young white boy and a young black boy coming into the store together would be followed wherever they went in that store. I still remember the name of one of them, as well as the look she had telling us "Yeah, I'm standing here to keep an eye on you both." As an adult looking back on those times, I think, "How degrading!"

When we would walk down one of the two major streets in our town, William would point out how white adults would cross the street in front of us as we would approach them and how when he would say hello there would be no response. (I have also read about that in books by black writers on their accounts of the way life was when they were growing up.) That was bad, but the worst episode of racism that I ever experienced was in the summer of 1970.

William and I were part of a small group of boys who played ball on weekends and in the summer. I was eleven years old and played baseball from morning to sunset. William was thirteen years old and the only African American boy in that group. On the day that I'm remembering, it was getting late towards evening and we were playing at the far end of the Pacific Grove Junior High field away from Fountain Avenue. While we played on the grass, many people would walk around the track. During the game, one of the boys in the group used the F- word. A white couple in their late forties or early fifties was walking by and the man just went ballistic at guess who. Yeah, at the only black kid. He started yelling, "I own you!" By then, there was total shock on the faces of eight kids aged ten to thirteen. The guy had veins coming out of his face! The wife finally got him to move on and we went back to playing.

I wasn't feeling too good about what had just happened to my friend of seven years, and I would have been lucky if it was all over. However, fifteen minutes later, the Pacific Grove police walked towards us from the street side of the field. The officer was (yep, you know where this is going) walking directly toward William. He tried to grab him, and fell right on his backside while William said, "Come catch me, Porky!" and went running along the length of the field and out of sight. At that time, he was living on Fountain Street, just two blocks away.

The policeman wanted all our names and information about what had happened. I thought he should have been interrogating the man instead, so I went home to talk to my mother about it. She then went to check on William at his home and to talk to his mother. By then, there were three police cars at William's house. The policemen treated my mother very rudely. I've seen that happen whenever a white person comes to the defense of a black man or woman. I'm sure that when I was young, there were other episodes to which I wasn't privy. It still disturbs me that decent people are treated in such a way. I cannot change that. All I can do is to live my life on a daily basis trying to do the best that I can to add to the kindness in the world. I don't know how you can be human and not be bothered when you see injustice.

My mother passed away many years ago, and when I think about her I think about the gift that she left with me. She taught me a respect for humanity and the old adage of treating people as you want to be treated. Black and white just wasn't important! I'm blessed to be able to discuss these issues with my friend from those times, Dirrick Williams, a local author whom I've known since first grade and with whom I talk two or three times each week.

I also have the honor of knowing Hattie Williams, Dirrick's mother. She is a woman of great faith and a pillar of grace and dignity. All of the people I've mentioned who are from black families treated me very kindly and even fed me at their homes. Sadly, what comes with getting older is that my friends' parents are now leaving to their greater glory. They will not ever be forgotten.

Leon has valuable insights as he reflects on the impact that racism has had on his life.

Leon's thoughts:

In this moment, when I think about how my racial prejudice has caused me suffering in the past, I think that my ignorance and arrogance have been main ingredients. My ignorance perpetuates my separation from people of color. For example, "I thought I was not prejudiced; therefore I was not prejudiced." However, my subtle behaviors were not examined, and I became comfortable with separation because I did not feel separate. It has been a costly arrogance.

As I look back, I now see that any separation which prevents me from engaging in an empathic relationship or inhibits the interconnectedness of love and compassion is dangerous ground for permitting human suffering.

When resistance to racism begins in adulthood, it often begins with an intellectual decision. Bruce recognizes that there are many steps to take in undoing and unlearning racism. He remains humbled by the perceived challenges of years of racist conditioning. Yet, there is hope in his ability to not act on these conditioned thoughts. We all have to start with one small step.

Bruce writes:

As for me, even with the benefits of a good upbringing, a great education, extensive travel, and a variety of life experiences, I still harbor prejudices and stereotypes that I acquired decades ago, but I've learned to control them, not to let them take charge. Maybe that's the best we can do until we can share this planet without the overlays of race, religion, and nationality, until we stop raising our voices and fists in rage instead of lifting our voices in harmony: "and the world will live as one." Imagine!

Gregory honestly and unabashedly tells his story of redemption. His narrative is a poignant reminder that humans can, and do, grow and change. He offers a different perspective on the damage that racism can cause white people and, in his willingness to share, offers valuable teaching and learning for all of us.

Gregory's story:

My name is Gregory and I am writing this to share a little about my trouble with racism. I am twenty-one years old, and I will be released from the state prison on August 18, 2017. I was fifteen when I started getting into trouble—vandalism, fights, and drugs. In many places this would be normal, but in Pacific Grove, where I grew up, this was pretty intense. It wasn't too many years before I ended up in the California Youth Authority (CYA).

Now my parents raised me 100 percent in the best way possible. I had friends of many different ethnicities. But when I reached CYA with that (accepting) attitude, I became a target. I was told in CYA that you always stick with your own race in order to survive. A few months into my stay, I was sexually assaulted by two inmates of African American heritage. Now, this blew everything my parents had taught me and everything I knew myself out the window. It wasn't long after my release from CYA that I started affiliating with a white supremacy gang. I joined the gang for a sense of acceptance and protection. Throughout my "career," I clung to that sense of acceptance. Although I did not always agree with all that I was told to do for the gang, I pushed through whatever misgivings I had because I was not going to let my brotherhood slip away. It went against everything my parents had taught me about equality, but I still did it. I would go downtown and write racial slurs and talk mess to people of varied ethnicities. I was a typical white supremacist—young, troubled, confused, emotional, and scared.

I also completely stopped listening to anything my parents tried to tell me. I started doing drugs to be cool. The entire time that I was acting like this, I didn't notice the way that people looked at me. I made people I had known my whole life feel uncomfortable. I got upset at my old friends and went further into hate and drugs. I believe I have spent probably a quarter of my life in institutions of some kind since CYA, and I am about to spend the next four years, six months, in state prison.

Recently, I made the choice to get out of my gang. Towards the end of my "career," I noticed how my ways and attitude were making people act differently around me. People I had known my whole life stopped talking to me. As well, I have to admit that I knew the entire time that what I was doing was wrong and a cowardly way to live. I had just suppressed the knowledge. Eventually, it came to the surface that the way I was living was wrong.

I also am tired. Not so much physically, but emotionally and spiritually. I have lost many friends and associates to drugs and prison, and my friend Christopher Glenn was shot and killed in Seaside in 2009. My own family has stayed up many nights worrying about my safety. I am sad that it took me this long to get out, but glad that I did. All in all I am just tired.

I have also dropped the hate from my life. I have been trying to live my life the way my parents taught me, but through my diligence in making a train wreck of myself and my life, I am having trouble. I have tattoos that mean allegiance to the white power gang, and I see skepticism on my family's faces. I know they love me unconditionally, but I was out there and did some crazy things to them and others. I dropped the hate from my life to help move along my change from drug-addicted gang member to, hopefully, functioning citizen. The hate also changed me in ways I wouldn't have expected. I did not even recognize myself at times. I was scared that I would lose myself and so, after way too long, I dropped the hate.

All in all, I believe my own racism has hurt me deeply. Who knows how my racism has hurt others—white, African American, Japanese, Latino, etc. The bottom line: Hate is heavy and racism *hurts* everyone.

They (white supremacist groups) are so dangerous because of how stealthy and seductive they are. I feel awful about hurting myself with my own racism. I feel that I have burned many bridges and many people with the way I lived. Also, I feel I have betrayed my parents by hating and not living how they taught me, as well as actively trying to tear down some of the things they have accomplished with some of my actions. I truly feel sad, drained, and ashamed—astonished by how I used to live.

I would like to educate myself about my own multicultural heritage: French, Native American, Latino, and Irish. I have confidence today that I will get my life in order. It will be hard, but I can do it as long as I remember *we are all people and deserve* to treat everyone with equality in everything. I also need to remember that with each and every step I take on this road to change, my family and true friends will be there with me and will be trying to help me. I *need* to keep my ears open and my mouth shut. I need to listen truthfully to what my parents tell me.

With a decision to move outside of racial isolation, Robert began to free himself from fear imposed by misinformation about African Americans and to open the possibility of significantly enlarging his world.

This is Robert's story:

I grew up in Charleston, South Carolina, in the 1940s and '50s. During that time and throughout my college years, I had no real contact with blacks. We went to different schools, drank from different fountains, watched from different sections of the movie theater, sat in different sections of the bus, and lived in different parts of town. The only African Americans I knew were servants, aged family retainers who worked for subsistence wages or lived in garage apartments and did whatever was needed around the house. We never engaged in social interaction.

It was not until I moved to California in 1965 that I had any social interaction with African Americans. Even then it was at a distance, and nobody talked about what it was like to be African American, other than being oppressed and discriminated against. I moved from one racial stereotype to another: from the "nice but inferior" to the "unfairly treated" and "somewhat dangerous."

At some point I made a black friend, but George was a hipster and so "cool" it never occurred to either of us to talk about what his life in Los Angeles had been like. We just clicked and hung out and smoked dope together, living in the "here and now."

If I had thought about it, my assumption would have been that it would have been out of bounds for me to actually *talk* with a black person about what being black in America was like. I'd read about it, of course, and I have to admit that I was surprised at the level of anger writers like Baldwin or Cleaver expressed. None of the blacks I had known seemed to be anything like that. But to ask a black person about his or her life was as unthinkable for me as dating a black girl in high school would have been. Both were taboo, one because of segregation and the other out of some sense of propriety: wouldn't it be rude for me to probe into the life of a black person? Of course, this reticence was racist as well. It stemmed from an unconscious assumption that his or her life would be so different from mine that I really couldn't understand it and, furthermore, that he or she would be offended if I did inquire, since that would certainly have been seen as patronizing.

It came as a shock to me when, well into my sixties, I attended a diversity workshop led by Ann Jealous, Caroline Haskell, and two of their colleagues and was actually encouraged to ask black people about their lives. "You mean they won't be offended?" I asked. Ann assured me that the opposite might be true and that the most probable response would be one of welcome. And so I tried it.

There was a mixed-race couple living down the street from us in Pacific Grove, California. I knew Garry and Dianne, his wife, well enough to greet and chat as we accidentally met while walking past each other's houses. When I took the bull by the horns and asked Garry if he would mind my asking him questions about his life, he was welcoming. So, after we shared dinner at my home one night, I proceeded to "interview" him, asking about his family, his childhood, his teen years growing up in Pacific Grove, his interracial marriage, his mixed race children—in short, about everything I had assumed I should *never* discuss with a black person.

I guess what impressed me the most was Garry's complete openness and willingness to share his experiences, good and bad, about being black in a predominately white town. I believe he painted a somewhat rosier picture than the reality probably had been, but he seemed genuinely pleased that I was interested enough to ask. Turns out that blacks (like whites) enjoy getting open-minded attention.

Although I still have few black acquaintances, the experience cured me of my reticence to broach personal topics with them. What I learned was that Garry's world is certainly different from my world, but because goodwill prevailed, there was the possibility of connection far beyond what I had imagined. It is as if I now have an entire territory of experience that I can explore and learn about that had before been terra incognita. I am delighted with this discovery that a part of the human race that had been closed off to me is actually available if I step beyond the cultural and self-imposed limits of what was once considered possible and acceptable. My world has grown.

Tom tells a story about a time he had the opportunity to run with a group of small black boys, while on a trip to Louisiana. A bystander in the neighborhood interpreted this experience of fun and youthful innocence and curiosity as a potential racial conflict. It is important to remember the natural innocence and curiosity of children who are not yet deeply conditioned by racial attitudes. It is equally important to remember the innocence of adults when they are in new places, eager to explore and make connections.

Tom's story:

It was hot. I walked out of the lobby of the Holiday Inn in Bogalusa, Louisiana, and stepped onto the tarmac. I could feel the heat through the soles of my Adidas. The South was new to me. I grew up and was educated in Maine. South was Boston. As a sales trainee for a major chemical company, I went where they sent me, and they sent me where our paper mill customers were located.

Crown Zellerbach owned a huge craft pulp mill in Bogalusa that made boxboard and paper bags. The air smelled like rotten eggs. If it wasn't so hot, I could close my eyes and think I was in Rumford, Maine. Kraft mills smell like Kraft mills the world over. The air stank and the river was polluted. People had jobs, and in 1967 nobody cared about the pollution.

I had on white shorts, a tee shirt, and a new pair of running shoes. I liked to run. It relaxed me after a day of travel, kept my weight down, and made the post-run beer taste terrific. I stretched my calf muscles and hamstrings and left the hotel parking lot at 4:30 in the afternoon. I turned right and began slowly running along the side of the road with the traffic. The shoulder was wide and level. I picked up the pace as I acclimated to the heat and began to plot a course that would carry me three or so miles from and back to the Holiday Inn. It looked simple.

I planned to run a ten-minute-mile pace, east ten minutes, turn south, run five minutes, then west ten minutes, finishing north for the remaining distance to the hotel. I planned a loop in order to see more of the area than what would be available by simply running up and down the main street facing the hotel. This plan had always worked for me in other cities, and I had no doubt it would work in Bogalusa.

I ran smoothly, working up a good sweat and looking for a turn to escape the exhaust of passing cars. I picked a side street close to the ten-minute mark. There was no traffic, and I was able to move off of the shoulder and onto the pavement. The street was lined with single-family houses with small yards showing signs of children in residence. As I ran deeper into the neighborhood, the houses showed increasing signs of neglect and disrepair. Painted walls gave way to peeling white wash and then to grey weathered boards completely devoid of paint. Perhaps they had never been painted. Yards became more cluttered; porches sagged under the weight of washing machines, overstuffed chairs, and sofas. Driveways often held two or more old cars, one running and the others there to supply spare parts as needed. The houses sat on cinder block foundations. Tall grass and weeds grew under porches where the sun shown.

I began to notice that the road had curved. Rather than heading due south, it veered off and showed no sign of side roads that would lead me west, as I had planned. I began to wonder if I should turn around and retrace my path when I heard the sound of someone running behind me, several someones. I turned to see a group of black children coming up behind me. There were six of them, and they looked to be between eight and fourteen years old.

"You a ballplayer, mister?" the oldest looking boy asked.

"No, I answered, "I'm a salesman."

"You look like a ballplayer," he said. "Why you running?"

"I like it," I told him.

"Can we run with you, mister?" he asked.

"Sure," I replied.

I was glad to have the local company and asked him how I could get back to the main road. He told me there was a road up ahead and he would show it to me. We ran for a few minutes and the younger boys, tired or seeing that I wasn't a ball player and no one of any importance, soon began dropping off, leaving me alone with my guide. True to his word, he hung with me until he pointed out the road I was to take, then slowed and turned back toward his neighborhood. I thanked him. He waved. I picked up the pace, following his direction and soon finishing my run in front of the Holiday Inn.

As I walked through the parking lot to cool down in the still warm afternoon air, a police car pulled abruptly into the entrance drive and approached me. The officers, one black and the other white asked me if there was any trouble. "No trouble," I replied, "Why do you ask?"

The black officer spoke. "Well," he said, "We've been following you for the last few blocks and couldn't catch up through traffic. We got a call from a woman saying that a white man in his underwear was being chased by a gang of kids through one of the worst neighborhoods in Bogalusa." I laughed and explained how the kids had joined me and been helpful. He didn't laugh, no doubt because there were better things a couple of officers could do than look for a Yankee salesman running loose in their precinct. He advised me to run circles in the parking lot instead of causing concern to old women. I assured him I would cause no more concern, since I would be leaving town the next afternoon.

That was not the only time I visited Bogalusa, a city I learned had a history of poor race relations, but it was the only time I ran with the kids and enjoyed the raceless innocence of curious children no different than children anywhere. I hope some of them remember the experience as well and as fondly as I do.

Bettina has been an activist, an author and a teacher for most of her adult life. In a brief interview with Ann, she offers wisdom gained from active engagement in cross-racial relationships.

Interview with Bettina:

Ann: How is racism harmful to you?

Bettina: Racism colors everything about everything in the United States and the way people think—especially in the political arena. It has a negative effect on white students. I am a teacher, and I have to find ways of introducing history that don't make them defensive. I have to extend compassion, rather than blaming them. I'll give you an example so that you'll understand what I mean.

I have a colleague in the Jewish Studies department who is teaching European Intellectual History. He said, "You cannot teach that subject without addressing the issue of anti-Semitism, but it is done all the time by historians."

The same thing is true about U.S. history. Everything is related to the slave trade and slavery and what happened after the betrayal of Reconstruction that legalized segregation and encouraged and fomented racist violence that is part of the deepest fabric of American life.

When I refer to the "betrayal" of Reconstruction, what I mean is that at the end of the Civil War the question facing the nation was what was going to happen to the newly freed three million and more former slaves. The Radical Reconstructionists in the U.S. Congress wanted to extend voting rights and citizenship rights to all "males over the age of 21 and regardless of previous conditions of servitude." That was the language that was used. Such legislation, which initially passed in Congress, was fiercely opposed by the former slaveholders, many of whom re-armed themselves and began a reign of terror against the black community. After all, I explain, the Ku Klux Klan was founded in Pulaski, Tennessee, in 1866. Meanwhile, as long as federal troops remained in the South, and as long as the Freemen's Bureau was able to operate, even in limited ways, rights of citizenship were legally and politically claimed by black men and women. For example, black women sued to have their children returned to them when former masters tried to "apprentice" them back onto their plantations into virtual slavery. And when black women were sexually assaulted, as they frequently were by white men, they pressed charges against them whenever and wherever they could. Meanwhile, black men exercised their right to vote and tried to form coalitions with poor whites, and these were sometimes successful. Thus, black men were actually elected to Congress, including the United States Senate, and to various state offices.

After Lincoln was assassinated and Andrew Johnson came in as president (he was from the former slaveholding state of Tennessee), federal troops protecting the former slaves were gradually withdrawn. The process was completed in the 1877 presidential election when Rutherford B. Hayes, in a close contest with Samuel Tilden, agreed to withdraw the rest of the troops in exchange for Congressional approval that he claim the White House. After this, a brutal system of segregation was relentlessly enforced. That is what I mean by "betrayal."

I also ask my students to think about why it is that most of them have never been introduced to this history, why they don't know it, and what it has to do with how they think about politics and candidates and issues in the United States today. Sometimes my white students are particularly outraged that this history has been denied to them. They feel it personally. They begin to see the ways in which racism became such a pervasive ideology.

The assumption of white superiority, for example, is not even considered when many people think about voting rights or all of these new state legislative initiatives to restrict access to voting. Nor do most white people, including those on the Left, think about the racism that has so deeply affected the terrible discourtesy and contempt with which President Obama has been treated, especially in Congress, and most especially by its so-called Tea Party representatives. Even mainstream Republicans have participated in this. While I share some of the disappointment that many of us feel about the Obama presidency, it is important to think about the special effects of racism with which he has had to contend.

In addition, of course, racism causes people of color pain every day. It causes me pain to think about that. I'm trying to help. In my everyday life, I do all that I can. As a Jewish person, I know how much pain and suffering is felt. The Middle East crisis is not understood because of a lack of understanding of anti-Semitism and Jewish history and a lack of understanding of racism and Palestinian history.

African American culture, Chicano Latino culture and Native American culture offer rich and beautiful gifts: music, poetry, ideas, and inspiration. These could be shared if more white people would learn to listen.

Ann: What was it like for you to grow up with parents who had African American friends at a time when segregation and de facto segregation were both so common in this country? What lessons did you learn about difference from living in that environment as a young child?

Bettina: I was raised in New York in the 1950s. My parents were very prominent members of the Communist Party, and my father was a prominent historian of black history. As a result, as a child, I was surrounded by black people who were from both the intellectual black community and the Communist black community. W. E. B. Du Bois, Shirley Graham Du Bois, Paul Robeson, Eslanda Robeson, William L. Patterson, Alphaeus Hunton, Louis Burnham, John O. Killens, Charles White, Doxey Wilkerson, Dorothy Hunton, Alice Childress, Beah Richards, Louise Thompson Patterson, Dorothy Burnham, Elizabeth Catlett, and Yolanda Wilkerson all attended my parents' parties at our home.

Although many aspects of my family life were difficult, black people gave me unqualified love and joy as a child. This was especially true of Dr. and Mrs. Du Bois, with whom my father worked very closely. They were each so kind to me, so respectful of my ideas and of my questions. It left such a deep joy within me so that when I see pictures of them now or think about them I am flooded with happiness. As a consequence, I grew up with enormous respect and love for black people that is emotionally embedded.

As I got older and understood the pain of racism, I felt a deep emotional need to give back for the love that I received.

Ann: How were you able to hold onto those lessons as you grew older and your world grew large enough for you to have to interact with people who did not have attitudes that embraced racial difference?

Bettina: I was friends with black children whose parents were Communists and activists in the black community: Angela Davis; Margaret Burnham; Mary Lou Patterson. When Angela was arrested and facing murder charges, I thought that a priority in my life was to help to free her. That immersed me in a vast international audience led with great brilliance by black people in the United States. In that way, I learned that one pernicious form of liberal racism was to support civil rights while also wanting white people to lead. Many white people felt they had to lead the movement if it was going to succeed, that somehow black people weren't really competent to do it. However unintentional, it is a way of enforcing the idea of white superiority.

Ann: You have spent most of your life actively fighting for racial justice. How has the struggle served you? It is very hard work—and often, thankless. Why do you continue?

Bettina: In my experiences working for Angela's freedom and in support of black liberation, I received many personal gifts of great benefit to me—about compassion, perseverance, and intellectual understanding. For example, Angela gave me my first introduction to feminism in a jail cell before her trial. We were both twenty-seven years old. A few years later, I went to graduate school to study black women's history and to teach women's studies.

Even when I encountered people with very racist attitudes, I did a couple of things: When I was a young adult, I argued. I wasn't very skillful at that and I got too angry. So, I wasn't effective in changing attitudes. It made them defensive.

In the early 1980s, while teaching at the University of California, Santa Cruz, I encountered a Chicana student who was very angry with me after a class presentation in which I did not adequately present Chicano people. Because, by then, I had started to gain a little understanding of Buddhist compassion, I did not get defensive. I said to her, "You are right." I know she was startled by that, but she told me later how much she appreciated it. Then she came to my office hours and began to teach me about her experience as a Chicana growing up in a poor, rural community, and I began to study.

The same thing happened with Jewish students who were angry with me because of how I taught about Jewish women and anti-Semitism. I said, "Talk to me." I met with a dozen of them—beautiful young women. Then I talked to my teaching assistants about internalized oppression and gave my first extended lecture on anti-Semitism. One of my TAs (Teaching Assistants), a Puerto Rican woman, sat first row and center during that lecture, emanating love for one hour and forty-five minutes to support me. After class, she said that she understood internalized oppression and thanked me. And I thanked her.

Ann: How has your history of interracial experiences impacted your own children's attitudes about race, racism, and racial difference? What is your expectation of the attitudes that your grandchildren will hold as they age?

Bettina: My son, Joshua, teaches English as a Second Language (ESL) to immigrants from all over the world and is an exceptional teacher. The vast majority of those immigrants are, of course, people of color. My daughter, Jenny, works at a nonprofit organization that focuses on access to science education for Chicano and Native American young people. She is their senior editor and does exceptional work. My grandsons are very loving and accepting of children from many different communities, and I expect that will continue to be true.

Ann: Bettina, thanks so much for the interview.

Bettina: Totally my pleasure, Ann.

Greg's story illustrates the growth in understanding and awareness that can come from even one personal experience of heartfelt activism.

Greg shares:

I was arrested in Arizona, on July 29, 2011, for blocking a thoroughfare while demonstrating in the street against the Arizona Support Our Law Enforcement and Safe Neighborhoods Act (SB 1070 law) that went into effect that day. I showed up with 120 other Unitarian Universalist ministers at the request of colleagues serving there. We were being called to witness the racial discrimination and cultural tension that surrounded the immigration issue.

Eighty-three of us were arrested, including forty from my denomination. I hadn't gone to Arizona planning to demonstrate or to get arrested; I just went to learn. I met with Catalyst, an anti-oppression group, and Puente, a Latino rights organization. We studied the immigration issue, the laws, and the impact they would have on the Latino community. Still undecided on my plan, I attended the morning interfaith service at a downtown church where the local Catholic bishop preached a sermon reminding us that Jesus was an undocumented worker with a message for people to love beyond regional, religious or racial affiliations.

Several hundred Unitarian Universalists poured out of the church and marched to demonstrate at the courthouse wearing bright yellow "Standing on the Side of Love" shirts. We are a mostly white denomination, and we joined

1,500 demonstrators, mostly people of color. It was the look of surprise, amazement, and hope on the faces of so many Latinos that ultimately convinced me to stand with them in solidarity. They didn't know what to make of us. Neither did the media.

"You are not Latino. Why are you here?" they said, seeing my clerical collar.

I replied, "Because when fear gets written into law, someone has to stand on the side of love."

"There are hundreds of police with riot gear. Aren't you afraid?" they asked.

"Yes, I'm afraid. But I'm more afraid of living in a country where police stop and arrest people based on the color of their skin. I'm afraid of living in a country where those who stand in fear of discrimination are allowed to stand alone."

Having grown up in east Los Angeles, I thought I knew about racial tension. I had seen how immigration issues compromised families of many of my friends, and the unfair treatment Latinos got in school. I thought I knew what racism looked like and where it lived. In Arizona, I discovered that an entire jail could be filled with what I didn't know.

We've heard a lot about how undocumented workers come to this country out of arrogant disregard of the immigration system, but we fail to recognize that the people of Central and South America have been migrating back and forth for thousands of years—long before the United States existed.

We fail to realize that by diverting the Colorado River, we destroyed much of the farmland in Mexico. We fail to consider the impact of flooding Mexican markets with the U.S. surplus of corn and the effect of U.S. corporations building factories in Mexico that they fill with cheap labor as they dump toxic waste and remove Mexican products and profits. We don't think about how drug cartels from Mexico, responsible for unspeakable crimes, exist only because the market for the drugs is here.

In the twenty-seven hours I spent in jail, I saw three prisoners of color for every white prisoner. I saw that they were treated with more aggression and intimidation. I saw that they were still in jail when we were released. I learned more about immigration and institutional and systemic racism in those two days than in my lifetime of reading newspapers.

Next week, I will be asked how I plead and I've decided to plead "not guilty." I don't have delusions of grandeur that my case can fix a broken immigration system, but I know that it can continue the conversation. It can give strength to people who are too frightened to speak out. I hope it can also help good sense become a little more common.

Dwight tells of lessons learned from his family and experiences as a young priest that influenced his ability to act courageously in the face of racism.

This is Dwight's story:

The seeds sown in our childhood experiences often set the stage for the development of our attitudes, preferences, and prejudices.

My grandmother was a significant influence in my life. She liked people and always found the diversity of them interesting. She had divorced my grandfather in 1906 and later married a man with a Spanish surname, thus personally experiencing the prejudice of family and friends. He was fifteen years her junior. When asked why she married him, she said, "He makes me laugh."

I grew up in northern California at a time when there were no black families, Asians were prohibited from staying overnight anywhere in the county, and the local Indian tribes were considered and treated as inferior and incompetent. My father agreed with this view. My siblings and I felt that the only way "to hold our own" was to take an opposite view on almost everything my father proclaimed. We were rarely allowed to "win," and this situation continued far into our adult lives. His outspoken racism gave rise in his three children that he was probably as wrong about this as he was vocal. Fortunately, my mother felt differently about people and race.

I became an Episcopal priest in 1955. In the summer of 1963, my assistant went to Selma, Mississippi, to register black voters. It was the summer before the march to Montgomery, Alabama, and his recounting of experiences there was both enlightening and scary. Bishop James Pike, the bishop of California at that time, was in the forefront of the civil rights movement, and he arranged that many clergy of his diocese should go to various portions of the march with Dr. King. I came to the conclusion that I would not be able, in good conscience, to preach if I did not take part in the march. So I went with a group to Washington, D.C., to lobby congressmen from California. Following that, we took a train to Atlanta, Georgia, and then on to the outskirts of Montgomery, Alabama, where we disembarked to join the marchers for the last two miles into Montgomery. We were an amazing assortment of people walking through the countryside and black neighborhoods—white and black middle-class folk, astounded at the poverty of these neighborhoods.

We became the several thousands of people gathered in front of the Alabama capitol building to hear a major address from Dr. King and several speeches from other leaders of the civil rights movement. At the close of that session, those of us who were to take the train to Washington, D.C., walked back through the city, carefully and quietly, ignoring catcalls from various people along the way.

I remember being inspired by Dr. King, encouraged by the young and old, white and black marchers, and frightened by the atmosphere of the city and the hatred expressed by ordinary people. I have always been grateful for the experience and for my decision to participate in that dramatic and fateful moment. That decision and action changed me, and it was instrumental in changing the thinking of a few of my family and several of my congregation, although my father could find no reason to explain why I went to Alabama to march with Dr. King.

The "change" in me through this experience was reflected in my becoming actively outspoken on the issues of racism. When the Reverend Morgan Tabb, an ordained African American Episcopal priest, came into my life at St. Mary's, there was never any doubt in my mind about including him in our ministry.

Morgan Tabb came to California from the East Coast to be the vicar of St. Cyprian's Church in San Francisco. The congregation was black and it was a "mission church," meaning that the diocese had to support it financially. Morgan was married and had a family, and his stipend was meager. He went to work for the San Francisco Juvenile Justice system as a probation officer to supplement his income. The rumor surrounding his leaving St. Cyprian's was that the bishop would not allow him to have a second job if he was to remain a vicar.

He worked for thirty years in the criminal justice system with juveniles. During those years, I often encountered him at diocesan events.

Upon Morgan's retirement in the early seventies, the then bishop of the Diocese of California offered him a position as vicar to St. Matthias Church in Seaside. Morgan thought of it as a ministry among blacks, but instead it was a difficult mixture of peoples with the primary thrust of work to evangelize the local black culture. Morgan came to see St. Matthias's ministry as incompatible to his experience and age and resigned as vicar.

At that point he appeared at St. Mary's by the Sea in Pacific Grove, where I welcomed him as a colleague and a friend. He offered to assist me in the ministry at St. Mary's, and I accepted with gratitude. He gave generously of his time and talent, despite the fact that there were no funds available to pay him. He became a valued and loved part of the parish ministry. He preached and either led services or assisted in them; he had a pastoral ministry of visitation, including the local hospitals. Morgan was with me in this capacity for about six years. Morgan stayed on with us as an admired and loved elder cleric until his death.

A picture of Morgan Tabb hangs in Clay Hall in the gallery of clergy who have served St. Mary's by the Sea since 1886.

Susan's story encompasses personal harm as a result of racism, as well as a broader perspective on how racism impacts the entire society and communities in which we live. As the wife of an African American man and the mother of mixed-race children, she has firsthand knowledge of how racism has affected her family. She is also clear about the ways in which she has been hurt. While she unravels many layers of the hurt caused by racism, she also weaves in ways to address the issues that she identifies.

Here is Susan's story:

In war, collateral damage describes the unintended harm that is caused to those who are near the target of the attack. Racism is a lot like that. We who are white may not be the targets, but we are harmed. There are things that we know, but we don't realize until someone asks the question. And then we say "Oh, yes. . . ." The question "How does racism harm white people?" is such a question.

So when "How does racism hurt white people?" is asked, an answer, though not previously pondered, is easy to generate.

The most immediate thought may be of personal hurts, but there are many layers of harm. The image I have of the impact on me is like an onion with the layers peeling back to the core of personal hurts. But we all function in a bigger context, so we are also affected by the harm caused to the outer layers of the society and economy as a whole.

It seems counterintuitive to imagine that we white people are harmed by the oppression against another group, but it takes just a moment to see the many ways. One glaring example is the justice system. The cost is economic, about $40,000 per year per prisoner. There is data in a 2011 report from the NAACP that supports the observation that racism hurts all people by overfilling our prisons: "The well-documented disparities in enforcement of our drug laws reveal that current drug policies impact some communities more than others. While Americans of all races and ethnicities use illegal drugs at a rate proportionate to their total population representation, African Americans are imprisoned for drug offenses at 13 times the rate of their white counterparts." Additionally there is a strong correlation between race and the use of crack cocaine. The sentencing for crack has been far more harsh than for the powdered form of cocaine. The latter often lands someone (usually white) in rehab, rather than prison. So, while people of color are disproportionately incarcerated, we white people, along with everyone else, pay.

Our tax bills remind us of the harm that racism does. Moreover, there are communities that border ours where disparities in enforcement and sentencing result in a near-absence of men and fathers of color. Many have been incarcerated for crimes that might result in probation in another kind of community. Without men and fathers, youngsters may stray further. Again the cost is economic as well as to the heart and health of a community.

The layers go deeper to my work as a school psychologist and parent educator. This brings me into schools in all kinds of neighborhoods. I try to help the parents I train in the gated housing developments to see that there are no gates strong enough to protect their children from the children who have grown up in communities where racism has limited their opportunities. My work brings me into places where the terrible intersection of poverty and racism is the toxic stew that many of the youngsters I work with grow up in. I see potential in these children, but I know it will be hard to realize that potential. I, this white person, may be affected by the absence of the great doctor, teacher, or public servant one of these children could become. A few make it through, but those exceptions are sometimes used to judge the others. I am hurt economically, I am hurt when youngsters do not grow up to contribute to the community, and I am hurt personally because of my attachment to these children. I try to help and do what I can, but there is a tall barrier that, even with my help, they cannot climb. So I stand with them, sad, at the bottom of this wall. I am hurt by seeing those I care for in a bad situation that I cannot change.

The next layer of personal is in my family. Unlike many families, mine was not an obstacle to a mixed marriage. My husband had been a friend for years before we got married, and so my family was aware of what a fine person he was. For my family, the only wish was that my husband be a good person who would treat me well. They got their wish. Mine is a "no-drama" family, and that approach applied to my marriage as well.

Another layer of this situation was not always so comfortable. As the wife in a racially mixed couple, over the last thirty years I have often been the only white person at various family and social events. While times have changed over the years, there have been several situations in which my presence was clearly not welcome. It was not just me; it was the symbol of me, the symbol of the oppressor. And what's more, I had done the unforgivable; I had "stolen" an eligible black man from the community. While the hurt I experienced was not deep, it was there.

Then to the deepest level, to the people I care most about, my husband and children. My husband is a successful man, a college teacher, a person of great stature and dignity, but it has always hurt to know of the childhood experiences and the indignities with which he has dealt.

In the course of our years together, there have been small hurts as I have made plans for trips or vacations. I wondered if we would be welcomed at various places or if there would be some awkwardness or insult. I wished that

I could call places first and say, "Oh, by the way, are you going to have any trouble with a mixed couple?" A silly wish. It couldn't happen. So instead I have sometimes made choices to not go certain places or take part in certain events. I might have been wrong, but I could not take the risk that something special would be ruined by a racist gesture or attitude. Though small, the hurt has been in the form of limits I placed upon us to protect us.

Perhaps the deepest hurt has come from situations my children have had to experience. In my work with parents, it is clear that we can endure many things, but we cannot endure seeing our children hurt. My husband and I taught our children, by word and example, not to see racism at the base of every insult or problem. I have seen, in my work and life, that the misperception of racism can be as limiting as racism. It is better to understand that what is clearly racist usually comes from ignorance and fear and it is definitely better to miss an insult than to perceive one where it does not exist. In spite of this understanding, there have been incidents that were hard to ignore.

Many youngsters of color have had the experience of "driving while black." Our son has had a few of these. The most troubling incident occurred when he was a teenager parked in an upscale neighborhood in an old family station wagon getting correct directions to a party. He and two other boys of color were pulled from the car, handcuffed and pushed on to the curb without explanation. These three six-footers were then pushed into the back of the police car. Our naïve son said, "Sure you can search the car." He had nothing to hide and was probably scared to death. He didn't realize that one of his passengers had poured a few ounces of his dad's liquor into the water bottle in his gym bag. The anxiety and worry over that incident stretched on for months until the hearing. The police officer did not show. However, the hurt and worry consumed us for many months.

In spite of training our children to not perceive racism where it doesn't exist, there were incidents. As racially mixed children, there were situations in which teachers had an agenda or a worldview that did not include a child of color writing so well or being so capable.

Our daughter does not look back at her school experience with any clear memories of prejudice, but I believe, even at my most objective moments, that her shyness was often misperceived as a lack of ability. I wonder if her strong abilities in math would have been recognized and encouraged if she were a white child.

The hurt for what our children had to deal with reared its ugly head again last winter when my son went through a big paper purge and threw out lots of old school assignments. As I dumped the bags into recycling, I came upon a wonderful little book he had done for history in middle school. He was to write about an historic event for each letter of the alphabet and illustrate it. I looked through with great appreciation for his lettering, pictures, fine descriptions, and beautiful penmanship. Then, on the last page, the grade, C-, and the comment, "Nice illustrations, but those don't seem like your words." They were indeed his words, every one. The hurt of that year resurfaced—the hurt of my son being the "usual suspect" and hearing from other parents that he got in trouble for things other kids got away with. It hurt to hear from other parents that their children had told them how biased the teacher was against my child. I will never know for sure where her prejudice came from, but I do know how much it hurts to have someone you love misjudged or prejudged, regardless of the reason.

It is so important that all children have sources of feedback that are objective and valid. When they are not, the risk is that even the legitimate feedback might be ignored. It hurts to relive that year and the hurt of wondering stays with me. I look back and wonder not just what I could have done, not just what might have been, but what was. So, I peel the layers back from the bigger society with cultural and economic problems caused by racism to knowing that in schools there are young people who could solve our health and energy problems if they were in a society where the color of their skin did not matter one bit. In our society, it does matter, and so we white people lose. The layers go to the children I've worked with and the harsh situations that they live in where poverty and racism are intertwined.

The deepest layer is my family. All families have their challenges and their joys; mine is no different. But all of us, whether we are close to someone of another race or not, need to operate from a place of enlightened self-interest. The end of racism will benefit all, white people as well as people of color.

In reading more of the story Brenda began in chapters 1 and 5, we learn of the ways in which she has resisted the racism of her homeland of South Africa in order to heal the emotional wounds it created and to ultimately come to a place of self-acceptance and love.

Brenda's story continues:

"Mother's failing, come quickly": four words that in 1977 propel me across continents and hemispheres for over thirty hours. Lacking anchor in time or space, I move in a dislocated daze through Jan Smuts International Airport in South Africa. Approaching the desk of the immigration officer, my skin crawls with shame that I am coming back when I had sworn to never return. I am so ashamed of my country that when Americans ask, "Where are you from?" I counter their question with intentional deceit, "Where do *you* think I'm from?" I will agree with any of their outlandish guesses, be it Scotland, Sweden, Australia, Wales, Germany. "Oh, yes, of course. How clever of you."

Somewhere over the South Atlantic a wave of homesickness hits me with a visceral longing to feel the red-brown soil, to smell the acrid ozone of summer lightning. The accents of voices here echo my own, yet I feel alien, unwelcome. I dread my turn, anticipating the sneer of disdain from an Afrikaner who will recognize me as a fugitive from the Apartheid regime, someone he will consider too cowardly to stand and fight for white survival against the coming black tide. I hate him on sight, that burly red-faced racist, so like the boys I used to dance with in school. The official gives me a stern once-over as he takes his time inspecting the details of my passport.

Then his face breaks into a wide smile. "Welcome home, Vrystaat se meisiekind," he says—welcome home, little girl from the Free State. And I burst into tears. The unexpected kindness of that moment of grace reminds me that compassion and generosity are still possibilities. I let the crowd wait as I sob, struggling to smile back at his benevolent face.

I go home, wanting reconciliation and closure; I find nothing has changed. I dared not expect to receive my parents' blessings, but I did hope for some mutual understanding. My father smolders, remote and distracted. My mother in her morphine-induced state has become yet more paranoid. Accusing me of poisoning her food, she refuses to eat. "Don't bother," offers the doctor, "It will make no difference anyway." Sighing as he leaves the house, he remarks, "She's a difficult woman." "A difficult mother," I add to myself.

We interact like strangers, barely civil, or at best, grope for pleasant memories only to discover that even our recollections lack congruence. The vulgar personal odors of her morbidity frame my days, and I grieve as much for the mother-love I never received as much as for her imminent death.

I jump at the chance to escape when the mother of my old school friend invites me to tea. I meet Lillian on the veranda of the King George V hotel on the Durban esplanade and ask about Denise's life in Australia. Denise was my very first friend and I had not seen her since her family moved away when we were eleven-years-old. The waiter, an older black man in starched white, approaches with the silver tray loaded with tea and coffee. Lillian chooses tea, I coffee. Without a word, the waiter hands her the tea. He then raises the coffee pot.

"With cream?" he inquires, and I nod. He pours cream and then coffee into my cup, saying with the smallest of smiles and only a trace of irony in his voice, "Yes, ma'am, a little of you and a little of me. Thank you, ladies." With a small bow, he leaves us speechless. After a moment, we burst out laughing, realizing that with Lillian's British accent and my American, this man of courage and wit assumed he was dealing with women who might sense the absurdity of apartheid's racial laws.

Six weeks later I receive my father's telegram: "Mother died last night. Don't come home." Eighteen years later, only after the elections in 1994, can I willingly admit that I am a South African, white in the Rainbow Nation.

As Bob continues his story from chapter 3, he speaks of the shame he carried, his sadness and his outrage, and his gratitude—all of which led him to heroic actions in the long and continuous struggle for racial justice.

Bob writes:

I could not escape a sense of loathing for myself, and eventually the adults around me, while learning of the lynchings that occurred around me as a child.

Why didn't they take a stand against vigilante lawlessness? Where were people who respected law and order?

Our extended family of Zellners and Hardys certainly knew about Claude Neal and other racial murders in our area. Much of the drama took place in Chipley and Marianna, a short distance across the state line in the Florida Panhandle. Mother had lived in both places when Grandpa Hardy served churches there. Both my childhood homes are near where Neal was lynched.

While attempting to plumb the intensity of my feelings about the "deep dark secrets," known by absolutely everyone, I have been reminded of the "undertoad."

Throughout *The World According to Garp*, a novel by John Irving, Garp teaches his children to respect the undertow at the beach. They imagine and come to fear the "undertoad," a fearsome creature inhabiting the depths of the nearby pounding surf waiting to snatch unsuspecting small people. For me, lynchings were more fearsome than the foreboding suggested by the "undertoad." Hanging people from bridges and trees was infinitely more terrifying, partly because it had no name—at least no name adults were willing to speak aloud. Nobody talked about it.

As a small child, feeling stripped of all protection and safety, I was terrified of forces and evils afoot in the world. Even Dad and Mom were powerless over them. Could even a child be ground up in the meat grinder of hate?

The sorrow I feel as a white Southerner deeply hurt by our system and philosophy of apartheid, extends to the little children who were taught, carefully taught, to hate. Those kids, "little lynchers to be," to quote poet Claude McKay, swarming around the torn body of Claude Neal and plunging sharpened sticks into his wounds, were wounded as surely as Claude Neal. How could the adults around me, my teachers, including ministers and Sunday school teachers, expect me to grow into a kindhearted, giving person dedicated to a life of serving others if I was nurtured in the midst of a lie? How could my church leaders not have risen up as one and demanded a halt to racial segregation and oppression?

When my father, Reverend James Abraham Zellner, broke with his father and left the Klan, his brothers never spoke to him again in life. Dad joined other white ministers in the Alabama West Florida Conference of the Methodist, later the United Methodist Church, to bring justice and Christianity to the church. Knowing that dissident ministers had always been run out of the South, they pledged not to leave the conference. Instead, they formed a secret group of radical preachers called the Andrew Sledd Study Club. They chose the name of a local Methodist minister and professor at Emory University who stayed in the South, after being fired in 1902, when he came out against the lawlessness of lynching.

My father and mother came a long way from their upbringing in the segregated South, and they suffered as a result of racism. However, our family has a happy ending dealing with race and its wounds. Quitting the Klan, my father was not content to be an average Southerner and hew to the middle of the road on race and its hurtful consequences. He had been an activist as a Klansman, and he became an activist in the civil rights movement. Working with Rev. Joseph Lowery in Mobile, where I graduated from high school, he participated in the peaceful integration of public buses and became a colleague and behind-the-scenes worker with Dr. Martin Luther King.

I have always been grateful that my parents traveled the long hard road to racial equality and did not teach me to hate people who are different from me. Unlike many of my peers in the South, I was spared taking in the poison of racial hate along with my mother's milk.

As an activist on the front lines of the struggle, I have learned that brotherhood and sisterhood are not so wild a dream as those who profit by postponing it pretend.

After becoming aware of the wounding impact of racism on one's relationships and spirit, it can take many years of conscious and conscientious intent to heal. Valerie has spent most of her adult life in that effort and even now, she says, "My deepest sadness is that I cannot be on top of all the ways in which I participate in a hierarchical process I abhor."

Valerie continues:

But I can continue to work at it. I can confront my own entitlement and intervene when I hear racial slurs. I can educate myself by reading books and seeing films about people of all ilks. I can work therapeutically with Caucasians and all people to acknowledge wounds related to inequality and injustice and to support racial inclusion in all acts of kindness and generosity. I can vote for minority politicians and those who support laws that represent all people equally. I can participate in actively avoiding adding to the future one more moment of pain or shame based on race, gender, class, or any difference by my privileged ignorance or irresponsible omission of diversity.

As Caroline shares an experience with a family member's unconscious and hurtful racism, she offers a model for supporting the growth of positive change with compassion and love.

Caroline writes:

After Gary and I were married and had bought and decorated our first home together, we looked forward to having my parents see where we lived. I will never forget their first visit. They wandered through our house looking around and then said, "Caroline, your house is so Japanese! What will you do with anything you inherit, given how you have decorated your house?"

Later that night, as Gary and I lay in bed talking, Gary smiled at me and said, "Honey, I don't really think that having a Japanese house is the issue. I think it is that your husband is so Japanese!" We laughed at that, but it wasn't really funny. I recognize how often we laugh as a way to cover up the hurt.

My decision to partner with a man of Japanese ancestry has been a wonderful and challenging life-changing experience. I am given ongoing opportunities to learn and teach about racism and the effects of racism in my own family. I am reminded about how important love and forgiveness are in the face of the terrible conditioning that we white people receive, a conditioning that seems to make us stupid when it comes to understanding racism! I also have the enormous privilege of maintaining loving and close relationships with my family, in spite of the mistakes they continue to make. As I unlearn my own racist conditioning, I too make mistakes. Therefore, I am humbled when attempting to educate my family. I know that people can and do learn and grow, so I hold my family accountable for continuing self-examination, just as I hold myself. I am deeply grateful for Gary's generosity, for he remains steadfastly committed, not just to me, but also to the belief that we can and will do better.

JT's voice rings true and clear as she describes the benefits of working for change.

JT asserts:

One of my favorite parts of the [anti-oppression] work is that it allows, even celebrates, the idea of making mistakes. To truly do this work, you are going to make mistakes. It can't be helped. Sitting on the sidelines, being careful, worrying that you'll offend and appear ignorant, or not reaching out and asking questions doesn't change anything. You have to invest yourself in rooting out the misinformation we've been taught about one another. You have to break the polite veneer of not knowing what life is like for each other. It takes work to be quiet and really listen to what people are sharing. It takes work to let go of our defense mechanisms and see where we play a part in the pain and inequity others face. But, if you do that work, the rewards are immense.

Afterword

As we read the stories, we noticed the prevalence of themes of separation, shame, guilt, silence, and sadness, as well as the various forms of resistance to racist conditioning that many of the writers employed. Although we separated the stories into chapters, nearly all of them were appropriate for more than one. Other oppressions (e.g., sexism, classism, homophobia, child abuse, and adultism) were frequently interwoven with racism.

Although some of the writers had thought deeply about racial issues before joining this project, very few had done so in relation to the ways in which they were personally hurt by living in a racist society. Even fewer had done so in writing. For most of them, writing a personal story for this anthology was a challenging and courageous task. Many expressed difficulty as they began to look at their feelings related to witnessing or actively participating in racist behavior.

One writer sobbed as she spoke of the pain she felt on unveiling incidents related to her father's racism. Another spoke of the hours it took her to write the first line of her story. Many needed ongoing emotional support as they uncovered painful and long-hidden memories. Several needed to tell their story to one of us before beginning to write. At least one prospective writer was motivated to begin therapy to deal with her confusion and pain about racism.

Leon wrote: "*I will try to continue . . . thank you for the nudge.*" Liz apologized in an e-mail to Ann: "*The reason I am willing to share the story is in the hopes of helping you with this book. I don't really want to share it if it is likely to put a barrier between us. I am a little worried about that, but I think you know what racism is and how prevalent it is even in the minds of the 'virtuous.' So I hope it doesn't create enmity between us but rather the trust that comes with honesty. If it helps you with your book, it will help the fight against racism, so good will come of it and that helps me overcome the fear of vulnerability. Do understand that it is difficult for me, and that I understand that hearing these stories comes at a cost to you too. I apologize in advance."*

Several people told us that they had stories to tell and were interested in writing—and never wrote them.

Caroline knew immediately that she wanted to participate in this project by writing about how racism has impacted her life. Yet, every time she started to even think about putting her thoughts down on paper, she quickly began doing something else. So, from the very start, she had to think about her resistance, ambivalence, and hesitation to write about racism and what she might do to help herself.

One of the ways that she avoids her feelings of shame, guilt, despair, and grief is by experiencing frustration and irritation instead. Constant immersion in personal, emotional material while working on this book resulted in an increased ability to be with and simply notice all of her emotions. Not run away from them or make them go away, not turn them into anger, but just be with them.

Another ongoing consequence for Caroline was the opportunity to continue to educate white people about the costs of racism for all of us. In many of her discussions with white people who were not part of this project was the quick assumption they made that the book was about how people of color had hurt white people. She was able, again and again, to correct the false notion of "reverse racism."

Our dedication to having these voices out in the world strengthened with every story that we received. It was a powerful experience for us both, often requiring great patience and compassion. Ann was deeply appreciative of Caroline's collaboration and of the ease in the teamwork. The benefit of a shared racial identity made it possible for Caroline to speak easily with some of the writers in ways that Ann could not.

There were also surprises along the way. Neighbors whom Ann had known for decades began to talk openly with her about racial issues. Relationships with long-term white friends became more real as their knowledge of this project lessened their fear of saying the "wrong" thing, and Ann's commitment to saying what is true for her broke the "racial" silence.

Nearly every writer expressed gratitude for the opportunity to tell a story and, for many, the writing was a cathartic experience. One wrote in an e-mail, "Thank you for giving these thoughts a voice."

The degrading and relentlessly dehumanizing evil called "racism" is an institutionalized system of economic and social oppression of one group of people by another. Such oppression is not possible without causing harm to the perpetrators. It is not possible to hurt others if you have never been hurt; we cause psychological and spiritual damage to ourselves whenever we are hurtful to others. It is neither necessary nor possible, unless one is blind or medically "color-blind" to miss color differences between people or any other beings. What matters is the meaning that we give to those differences. It is when those differences are tied to factors that determine success or failure, wealth or poverty, imprisonment or freedom, that they separate us from one another and create pain and hostility, fear and shame, guilt and grief. We see no way for racism to end until we all recognize that, in some way, it hurts everyone.

This anthology has focused on how the system of racist conditioning has damaged white people, as well as what can be done to heal from that damage. It is our hope that the reading of this book will contribute to conversations that bring people together, that it will inspire readers to tell their own stories, that the storytelling will encourage self-examination and compassion, help to heal our hearts, and increase motivation to save our humanity and our souls.

A Reader's Guide for Self-Reflection: Questions and Topics for Discussion

The following guide can be used in a classroom, in ongoing workshops that deal with issues related to living in a multicultural society, in book clubs, in groups of friends who are interested in exploring their own experiences with racist conditioning, or in therapy groups. If used apart from a group setting, we suggest that the responses to the questions be entered into a journal. It may serve to deepen the reader's connection to the storytellers. We hope that its use will be of service in the reduction of racism.

Chapter One

1. Anne, Brenda, and Bonnie were all traumatized during childhood by being separated from loving caregivers of African heritage. Have you ever experienced the loss of a person you loved who cared for you when you were a child? Describe that loss and how it affected you. Did you have an emotionally safe person with whom to share your feelings about that loss?

2. Maren's experiences in her grandparents' home included powerful lessons about race and class. What did you learn during childhood about race and class differences? How and by whom were you taught?

3. JT's parents were verbally and publicly supportive of racial equality while they treated their housekeeper in less-than-equal ways. What experiences did you have of your parents or other caregivers saying one thing and doing another when

you were a child? What impact did that incongruity have on you?

4. Both Natasha and Valerie experienced confusion and feelings of powerlessness when their parents did not adequately and honestly respond to their questions. When you think of your childhood, do you remember having questions that your parents were unable or unwilling to answer? If so, what were those questions? How did you respond to not having them answered?

5. Leslie wrote of a painful shift in her feelings toward her grandparents because of their racism. She also experienced pain when witnessing her black partner's mistreatment. What are your memories of witnessing or otherwise experiencing racial inequality?

6. Diana's aunt supported the continuation of racism as she attempted to protect Diana's reputation. What memories, if any, do you have of other people attempting to protect your reputation when you were a teenager or young adult?

7. If you are white and have childhood memories of people of color, what are they? Were they actively involved in your life? If so, what did you learn from them? What did your relatives teach you about people of color? What did you do with those lessons?

Chapter Two

1. Fred remembers a childhood in which he had to endure discomfort and confusion without having any adult comfort him or talk with him about his feelings. Jeanne also recalls feeling emotionally distant from her parents. Was that true for you? Were you allowed to openly discuss difficult or negative feelings when the subject was about race or racism? Who was there to help you work through those feelings?

2. Julianne and Caroline write of feeling a loss at "not having been raised in a more ethnically diverse community." If you grew up in a homogeneous community and share their feel-

ings of loss, what deprivation do you think you experienced? If your community was ethnically diverse, what do you think you gained from that diversity?

3. Deb relates a story about a white college student who was extremely distressed upon awakening to the ignorance created by growing up in de facto segregation. Describe the community or communities in which you spent your childhood and adolescence. Did all of your community members have the same racial identity? If not, what kinds of relationships did you have with those who had racial identities that differed from your own?

4. Rosi writes of her commitment to be an ally to people who are labeled as "different" or "outsider." Do you believe that we are "our brother's keeper"? If so, what people do you include in that belief? How do you put that belief into action?

5. Dana struggles with a fear of people of color. If you are afraid of people whose racial identity is different from yours, how were you taught to be afraid? What have you done about freeing yourself from that fear? If you do not have such fear, to what do you credit your sense of safety?

6. In what ways has the community of your childhood changed? What do you think is responsible for those changes? How do you feel about them?

Chapter Three

1. Liz recalls a childhood experience of being intentionally verbally hurtful to a black classmate. What are your experiences with name-calling? Can you recall a time when you deliberately and intentionally inflicted pain by using a racist epithet? If so, what was going on with you at that time? If you have ever been hurt in that way, did it have lasting impact? If so, describe how it affected you.

2. There were many unspoken rules about race in Lynne's household while she was growing up. What were the unspoken

rules about race in your household or family? How did they affect you?

3. Leon and Patricia have both developed a consciousness that examines their racist conditioning. If you have developed such consciousness, to what do you attribute that decision and ability?

4. Joe and Lynne both write of experiencing "white guilt." If you are white, what experiences, if any, do you have with feeling guilty about your racial identification? How have you been challenged by people of color in looking at your racist conditioning? How have you reacted to the challenges, and what have you done to alter the conditioning?

5. Molly's sense of entitlement was directly challenged by a black coworker, and that challenge led her to greater self-awareness. If you are white and have ever had feelings of entitlement or superiority because of your racial identity, what instilled these in you? How were you taught to think about people of color? Have your beliefs changed throughout your life? If so, how?

6. Although Bob's father paid a dramatically significant psychological price for his overtly racist behavior, Bob's story also speaks to the emotional toll of being his father's son. What psychological price are you aware of paying for your participation in a racist society? If you have had a "crisis of conscience," what have you done about it?

Chapter Four

1. Susan's childhood friendship with Andy Sanchez and Deborah's friendship with Darryl and David ended because of parental fear and racism. Has your parents' fear or prejudice held you back in any way? If you have ever had to distance or separate yourself from friends or family because of their racism, what did you do?

2. Carolee wrote of feeling angry because the possibility of having a Native American friend during her adolescence was

eliminated by her father's racism. If you had angry feelings regarding your parents because of their racism as you grew up, how have you reconciled this today?

3. Jerry's father prevented him from having black playmates when he was a child. If your parents attempted to control or determine your friendships, did this have to do with racial or class-based differences? How did this behavior affect you? What choices have you made today about your friendships?

4. The childhoods of Diane, Maria, and Jerry all included experiences with people who cared about them and who helped them feel safe with people of color. What are your early memories of knowing that there are people of different races? What did you learn about the value of social group memberships? What experiences do you have of adults in your life who attempted to help you understand racism or to feel safe with people whose racial identification differs from your own?

5. Linda's story includes her earliest memory of hearing a racist epithet. What memories do you have of learning racist epithets? Were they spoken in your home? What did you learn about the power of these words?

6. Deborah wrote of her grief about racism and of the intellectual, emotional, and spiritual work she has done and continues to do as she struggles to come to grips with its meaning in her life. What opportunities have you had to wrestle with race and racism? What do you need in order to do this work?

Chapter Five

1. Kate suffered great losses because her mother's "carried shame" made a secret of part of her family's racial identity for such a long time. If there are aspects of your social identity for which you feel shame, what are they? If you have received incomplete information about your heritage or if you learned

secrets about family identity late in your life, in what ways, if any, has racism been involved? How has that affected you?

2. Brenda wrote of feeling deep shame because of growing up in a racist home. If you are white, how have you received preferential or unearned privilege? In what ways, if any, do you feel shame about racism? What are you doing about that?

3. Jeffrey grew up in de facto segregation and was ignorant about racism until his last year of high school. How did you learn about racism? In what ways has it been invisible to you? If you grew up in a segregated community, what were the messages you received about people whose racial identities differ from your own?

4. Eilene, Diana, and Valerie all wrote about ways in which they have unintentionally participated in racist behavior because of their conditioning. If you are white, what remnants of racist conditioning do you continue to carry? What opportunities have you had to consider what it means to have your racial identification? As you think about it now, what does it mean to you? As was true for Eilene, if you are white and have employed people of color to work for you, describe those relationships.

5. Ann's student projected his deep feelings of shame onto all African Americans and made assumptions about the entire group as a consequence of his projection. What experiences, if any, have you had, with people projecting their emotional states onto you and making assumptions about your feelings and behaviors? If you have had such experiences, how have they affected you?

6. Paula and Elaine both learned important lessons from their relationships with African Americans. If you are in an interracial relationship of any kind, what have you noticed and experienced? What experiences have you had with subtle or not-so-subtle racism? If you are white, how has your life been affected by having relationships with people of color?

Chapter Six

1. Caroline wrote about the challenges of emotionally charged conversations in workshops related to multiculturalism. If you have ever attended a workshop or a class in which you were afraid to speak for fear of upsetting some other participant or student, describe that experience. What was it like for you?

2. Leon continues to feel shame about having been silent as an adolescent when he witnessed an act of anti-Semitism. How have you learned to keep quiet rather than speaking up? What prevents you from speaking out against social oppression? If you are white, how have you colluded with the system of racism that is currently in place?

3. Louise wrote of her regretful silence in not being able to confront her mother's racism. If you have been able to speak out against racism, what risks did you take? What gave you the courage to speak out and what have you gained, as a consequence of that courage?

4. Racism, sexism, and adultism intersected in Diana's high school history class, and racism and homophobia collided in Deb's place of business. What experiences have you had or witnessed where racism intersected with another social oppression? How did you deal with that? How did it make you feel?

5. As Sue reflected on the determination to free herself from racist conditioning, she wrote of the necessity of welcoming mistakes. What mistakes have you made as you have addressed your own or someone else's racism? If there is something that you would like to do over, what is it?

6. As Deb shared personal experiences and understandings about white violence, she asserted that "it is out of fear that we [white people] act as silent accomplices in the perpetuation of the mythology that names peoples of color as the

violent . . . ones in our society." What do you think about that assertion? If you are white, are there things about race that you pretend not to know? What are you doing about your unconscious racism?

Chapter Seven

1. Diana wrote about family members whose racism surprised and disappointed her. If your family has disappointed you regarding racism, describe the disappointment and the way(s) in which it has affected your relationships.

2. Leon's association with other professionals was negatively affected by his feelings about their racism. If racism has affected your personal and professional relationships, have you found ways of resolving the difficulties? If so, what are they? If you are white and separate yourself from other white people, how do you do that?

3. Caroline and Tom shared powerful illustrations of some of the challenges that a racist society presents for white people who are open to interracial friendship. What are your experiences of wanting to be connected to people of color and not being able to foster that type of connection? How was racism a factor?

4. Carol and Markie wrote of painful challenges that immigrants face because of racism. How did your family come to the United States? How did they assimilate? What were the costs of the assimilation? What were the benefits?

5. Judy and Gayle shared stories of romantic relationships that ended because of racism and of the grief experienced because of that loss. Have you had experiences with intimate interracial relationships? If you have ever ended a relationship because of racism, what happened?

6. Leatha's memories recall family relationships that contained racial conflict and prejudice, as well as fun and love and generosity. What feelings do you still wrestle with when you re-

visit past relationships that were affected by racism? If you become defensive during conversations about race, what triggers those feelings?

Chapter Eight

All of the contributors to this chapter wrote of ways in which they have resisted racism and/or acted to promote racial justice. For some of them, the commitment is new; for others, it has been lifelong. All of them have demonstrated courage.

1. If you and/or members of your family have experienced courageously standing up against racism, describe the experiences. What have been the consequences of those actions for you?
2. How have you resisted racist conditioning?
3. What childhood memories do you have of either witnessing racism or acting in racist ways? What did you do? As you look now, how do feel about your behavior in those situations? What support did you receive? What support do you wish you had received?
4. What parts of U.S. history are missing for you? What are you aware of not understanding? What do you want to learn about? How will you educate yourself?
5. If you are on a path toward healing from the impact of living in a racist society, what steps have you taken? What is your next step? Who and what do you need to consider as you take that step? What support do you need? What changes do you want to make?
6. If reading this book has been a valuable experience, how has it served you?

About the Editors

Ann Todd Jealous spent ten years teaching sociology, psychology, and women's studies classes and nearly thirty years as a marriage and family therapist. She is a founding member of the Monterey chapter of the National Coalition Building institute, a member of the ACLU, a life member of the NAACP and the chairperson of the Board of Directors of The Village Project, Inc., Seaside, CA, a nonprofit mental health center serving historically underserved populations.

Ann has been in an interracial marriage for forty-six years and has a daughter, Lara, a design consultant for Southern Journeys, a worker-owned cooperative that is part of the Southern Rural Black Women's Initiative for Economic and Social Justice; a son, Benjamin, the current president and CEO of the NAACP; and three grandchildren. She is the author of *A Peace Corps Experience: From Letters Home: Musings at Twenty-something* (2011) and lives in Pacific Grove, California.

Caroline T. Haskell, a board-certified and licensed clinical social worker, is the founding director of the Personal Growth and Counseling Center and currently oversees all of Health and Wellness Services at California State University, Monterey Bay. She is the campus affiliate director for the National Coalition Building Institute, an international leadership training organization based in Washington, D.C., whose mission is to reduce discrimination of all kinds, including intergroup conflict and violence.

Caroline has thirty years' experience providing program development and management, clinical/counseling services, psycho-educational workshops and training programs on diversity and multiculturalism.

Caroline is a white woman who has committed to unlearning her racist conditioning and actively practices being an ally to people of color. Caroline is in an interracial marriage of almost twenty years where her "whiteness" is regularly examined and discussed with her Japanese American husband. This is her first book. She lives in Pacific Grove, California.

About the Contributors

Alisa Fineman is a performing, recording, and award-winning singer and songwriter. In 2011 she won Monterey County's "Champion of the Arts" Award. Her most recent CDs are *Faith in Our Love* (2009) and *Closing the Distance* (2004). Alisa also serves as Cantorial Soloist for Congregation Beth Israel in Carmel, California. She performs in a variety of interfaith and cultural community settings at home and across the country. **See chapter 8.**

Anne Farrow grew up in the Deep South and now works from her home in Monterey, California, where she designs women's clothes from vintage lace and doilies. She has also been a teacher and volunteer for the Art of Living Foundation for fifteen years. She especially loves spending time with her family. **See chapter 1.**

Bettina Aptheker, a native New Yorker, has been a participant in movements for civil rights and social justice since the early 1960s. She is professor of feminist studies and history at the University of California, Santa Cruz, where she has taught for more than thirty years. She is also a faculty mentor for graduate and undergraduate students. Her most recent book is a memoir: *Intimate Politics: How I Grew Up Red, Fought for Free Speech and Became a Feminist Rebel* (2006). Among her other books is *The Morning Breaks: The Trial of Angela Davis* (1976; second edition, 1999). Bettina particularly enjoys playing baseball, coaching Little League baseball, and attending games of the San Francisco Giants with her grandsons. Opera and classical music in general bring her great pleasure. **See chapter 8.**

Bob Zellner of Alabama, a *Student Nonviolent Coordinating Committee* veteran, has been an organizer for fifty-two years. He recently moved to Wilson, North Carolina, from the Hamptons in Long Island, New York, where he taught history to college students. Working with Rev. Dr. William Barber, state NAACP president, he and other southern activists are currently establishing a college for political and human rights organizers, named for North Carolina native Ella Baker. Bob's 2008 memoir, *The Wrong Side of Murder Creek: A White Southerner in the Freedom Struggle,* has been optioned for a film by executive producer Spike Lee. **See chapters 3 and 8.**

Bonnie lives in central California. She has a master's degree in child development and has worked as a parent educator and children's librarian. She also teaches yoga and yoga philosophy. Gardening, crochet, and walking the beach with her dog bring Bonnie pure bliss. **See chapter 1.**

Brenda Aronowitz grew up in Bloemfontein, South Africa, under the apartheid regime and currently lives in Salinas, California. Her life has been an interweaving of her passion for education, young people, literature, and Africa. For many years she taught English and history at high school and college levels. She coauthored *Good Grief for Kids: A Manual for Hospice Volunteers* (no longer in print) and was a contributor to *English Literature with World Masterpieces* (1989). Since retiring, Brenda spends her time writing and traveling. **See chapters 1, 5, and 8.**

Brenda Feldman spent her childhood in New Jersey and Georgia. She has been in sales for many decades and has been an insurance broker since 1990. She currently lives in Newbury Park, California, where she is active in community affairs. **See chapter 8.**

Bruce Yasgur lives in Havertown, Pennsylvania, and Gouldsboro, Maine. After a thirty-two-year career as a high school and college teacher, he now works as an attorney and legal educator. With wife, Janice, and son, David,

Bruce enjoys hiking, rowing, attending concerts and theater, and frequenting and finding new favorite eateries. **See chapter 8.**

Carol Lynn McKibben received her PhD in history from the University of California, Berkeley. She is the author of *Beyond Cannery Row: Sicilian Women, Immigration, and Community in Monterey, California, 1915–1999* (2006), *Seaside* (2009), *Racial Beachhead: Diversity and Democracy in a Military Town, Seaside, California* (2012), and numerous articles in both scholarly journals and the popular press, including the local *Monterey Peninsula Herald*. Dr. McKibben is a lecturer in American history at Stanford University and teaches courses on urban California, immigration, and public history. She is the coordinator for the Public History/Public Service Program within the history department. **See chapter 7.**

Carolee Hill worked in the education field in California and North Dakota teaching reading and special need students for thirty-three years. Currently she lives in San Diego, California, and works on her childhood dream of becoming an artist. **See chapter 4.**

Caroline T. Haskell was born and raised in Arizona and now loves living by the ocean in Pacific Grove, California. She has worked as an administrator, educator, and mental health professional in the fields of higher education, health care, and human/social services for thirty years. She has authored and coauthored several training manuals for professionals and has been publicly recognized for her leadership on mental health issues and her clinical service work. She thrives on being outside in nature and loves long conversations with family and friends. She lives with her husband, Gary, and their dog, Musubi. **See chapters 2, 6, 7, and 8.**

Dana Francis has been a medical social worker since 1988. He currently works at a major medical center in San Francisco with men who have hemophilia. Originally from Massachusetts, Dana lives in Alameda, California, has two wonderful sons, and likes to ride a bicycle and play the guitar. He dreams of playing in Bruce Springsteen's E Street Band. "The rhythm guitar," Dana says, "would suit me just fine." **See chapter 2.**

Deborah Burke resides in Marina, California, and is a faculty member with the Service Learning Institute at California State University, Monterey Bay. Her teaching and research focuses on creating educational environments inclusive of the histories and cultures of a diverse student body and serving students and families from low-income and working-class communities that have been marginalized from educational institutions. She gets joy from her participation with "Youth Alive!," an afterschool program that serves a migrant farm working community in Soledad, California. She also enjoys art, yoga, and hiking with her dog, Eva. **See chapter 4.**

Debra (Deb) Busman is a writer and professor at California State University, Monterey Bay, where she codirects the Creative Writing and Social Action Program and serves as coordinator of service learning. A longtime activist in the Monterey/Salinas area, she has published poetry, short stories, and creative nonfiction, and recently coedited *Fire and Ink: An Anthology of Social Action Writing.* **See chapters 2 and 6.**

Diana S. Case, PhD, spent her youth in southern California, Texas, and Wisconsin and currently works as a clinical psychologist in Monterey, California, specializing in health, stress, trauma, grief, and self-empowerment. She also provides crisis response for businesses and community organizations, as well as for fire and police departments. Additionally, she provides disaster mental health services as an American Red Cross volunteer. Diana loves exercise, hiking, nature, travel, music, and dancing. **See chapters 1, 5, 6, and 7.**

Diane Cotton has worked as a teacher and guidance counselor for over thirty years. She retired in 2007, but continues to work part-time with high school students and elementary students exposed to violence. She practices Nonviolent Communication and yoga and enjoys gardening and spending time with her grandchildren. A native Californian, Diane lives in Seaside, California. **See chapter 4.**

Dwight Edwards is a retired Episcopalian priest who lives in Pacific Grove, California, and continues to officiate at weddings, baptisms, funerals, and occasional Sunday church services, as well as serving as chaplain for other retired clergy. Swimming is an important part of Dwight's life, as is traveling with his wife, Rosi, and singing in a church choir. **See chapter 8.**

Elaine, a psychotherapist, is a frequent public speaker who has organized conferences and served as a trainer on parent education; prevention, detection, and treatment of child abuse and neglect; and parenting issues for families with special needs children. She has also facilitated race relations study circles. Since retiring her hospital-based practice, she has worked in pastoral counseling and served as a board member for several child welfare agencies. She lives with her family in Manchester, Connecticut. **See chapter 5.**

Eilene is a pseudonym for one of the listed contributors. **See chapter 5.**

Fred S. Jealous is a teacher who grew up in Maine and who now lives in Pacific Grove, California. For the past twenty-five years, he has served as the founder/director of the Breakthrough Men's Community. That work includes a thirty-four-session workshop in which participants do a major reevaluation of the male role. He enjoys swimming, the pleasures of walking in a small town on the ocean, and spending time with his family. He has been married to Ann Todd Jealous for forty-six years. **See chapter 2.**

Gayle Ward Azevedo is a social worker with Kinship Center, a nonprofit adoption and foster care agency in California, and lead instructor for the Education Institute, where she teaches curriculum on the clinical issues involved in adoption, attachment struggles, and identity issues that come with loss of family and multiple moves. With her beloved husband, Pete, Gayle co-owns Happy Trails Wagon Tours, giving local wine tours in Carmel Valley. She loves their three children, six grandkids, and her horses and dogs and has great passion for the outdoors. **See chapter 7.**

Greg Ward is an ordained Unitarian Universalist minister whose sermons, stories, and editorials have been published in several different newspapers, magazines, and books. He lives in Manassas, Virginia, with his wife, Liz, and dog, Blondie. Greg has a passion for working with individuals and communities committed to cultivating right relationship in little and big ways. **See chapter 8.**

Gregory T. grew up in Pacific Grove, California, and now lives in a state prison. Before going to prison, he was involved in community service. He doesn't have many options now, so he currently spends lots of time drawing. He also likes to think of ways that he can make up for some of the wrong he has done. Gregory is glad that he is who he is but wishes that he could change the way that he has lived his life. **See chapter 8.**

Jeanne S. Holmquist grew up in Nebraska and now lives in Pebble Beach, California. She had a long career in education with a variety of posts, including principal of an elementary school in Pacific Grove for seventeen years. Currently she volunteers at Community Partnership for Youth, a program serving at-risk children and low-income and single parents. Jeanne also volunteers to speak at schools and service club meetings about Marian Anderson. Once a week, she takes her dog, an SPCA therapy dog, to three convalescent hospitals. **See chapter 2.**

Jeffrey Whitmore, a past member of the San Jose Newspaper Guild and the Writers Guild of America, West, has published thirty books for young readers under the pen name Prescott Hill and the humor book *English as a Second F*cking Language* (1995) under the pen name Sterling Johnson. His work has appeared in *Cosmopolitan*, the magazine of the *Sunday San Francisco Examiner*, and Rod Serling's *Twilight Zone Magazine*. His "Bedtime Story" is featured in *The World's Shortest Stories* (1998). Originally from New England, Jeffrey now lives and works in Pacific Grove, California. **See chapter 5.**

Jerry Lee Hill has worked in the business world for the last thirty years in areas ranging from production to customer service. He is now a chef in San Diego, California. Jerry enjoys spending time with his grandchildren. **See chapter 4.**

Judy Lewis is cofounder and board member emerita of the Chartwell School and was one of the first members and organizers of the Board of

Trustees of the Orion Academy. For thirty years, she was a private tutor. In 1998 Judy established the NLD Coaching Connection and became the creator, webmistress, and administrator of the NLDline website. Judy and her husband, Leland, live in California and have four daughters and eight grandchildren. She is an avid walker, reader, and mahjong player and is currently writing a book about nonverbal learning disorders. **See chapter 7.**

Joe Ruklick, who lives in Chicago, majored in English in college and studied literature because he enjoys stories. He was a basketball All-American and a charter member of Northwestern University's Athletic Hall of Fame. Joe played in the NBA from 1959 to 1962 and got the assist on the bucket that gave 100 points to Wilt Chamberlain. He has a master's degree from Northwestern, was a reporter and editorial writer for sixteen years, and still enjoys stories. **See chapter 3.**

Julianne Leavy, MFT(Marriage Family Therapist), is founder and executive director of Harmony At Home (HAH), a nonprofit counseling agency with a school-based program and the mission "to end the cycles of violence and abuse by empowering children and young adults with the knowledge, skills and confidence to lead healthy and productive lives." In 2003 Julianne wrote and published "The Innocent Victims," a handbook that looks at the effects of domestic violence on children and helps caretakers to understand and respond to their needs. Julianne resides in Carmel, California, with her husband and son. **See chapter 2.**

JT Mason has worked in public radio for twenty-eight years. A native Ohioan, she, her wife, and their daughter, as well as a household of animals, live in Carmel, California. JT is a glass artist, specializing in mosaics, and a teacher of religious education at the Unitarian Universalist Church of the Monterey Peninsula. **See chapters 1 and 8.**

Kate Spacher lives in Carmel Valley, California, with her partner and two dogs. Kate is a licensed clinical social worker and deputy director of a nonprofit mental health agency. Kate has been publicly honored for her work on fighting the stigma associated with mental illness. Kate loves gardening, walks in nature, and fun adventures with her three sons. **See chapter 5.**

Leatha Harris is now retired after a thirty-three-year career, first in nursing, then as a corrections officer for the California State Prison system. She lives in Atascadero, California, in the hills above the magnificent Central Coast, spending most days in the sparkling company of her four-year-old grandson. **See chapter 7.**

Leon has long been interested in deep listening and peaceful communication. Now retired from forty-five years of private practice as a marriage and family therapist, he continues to create and publish structured communication word play games that promote intercultural, intergenerational, interpersonal, and interfaith conversation. **See chapters 3, 4, 6, 7, and 8.**

Leslie Milliken, a retired printer, resides in San Diego, California, where she enjoys taking care of the home she shares with her partner. Leslie loves music, photography, cooking, and gardening. **See chapter 1.**

Linda Houghton Madsen grew up in Denver, Colorado, and now lives in Marina, California. In addition to teaching at the preschool, middle school, and high school levels, she has worked as a secretary, an intelligence analyst, a school district public information officer, and a writer, developer, and editor. Linda is passionate about peace and justice, languages and international relations, art and music, nature and the environment, walking and swimming, poetry and photography, and most especially, husband Roy, daughter Laura, and beloved family and dear friends. **See chapter 4.**

Liz (Elizabeth) is a web developer, IT manager, and Unitarian Universalist. She was born in Spain to a military family. Her childhood incident described in chapter 3 took place on an army base in Germany. Liz is fascinated by the way experience shapes wisdom and enjoys putting herself in the path of wisdom by the simple action of being open to unfamiliar experiences. **See chapter 3.**

Louise Barnard grew up in Wisconsin and now lives in Monterey, California, where she works as a psychotherapist/social worker specializing in psychological trauma treatment. Working part time, she also engages in her passion for art by painting, printmaking, and gardening. Her horse, Rocky, keeps her on her toes. **See chapter 6.**

Lynne Sexton lives in Pacific Grove, California, and is a certified public accountant. She is a former board member and volunteer for the Monterey County Chapter of the National Coalition Building Institute. She enjoys spending time with her two grandchildren, as well as cheering on her favorite baseball and hockey teams, reading, and walking. **See chapter 3.**

Maren Martin is a psychotherapist specializing in couples and sex therapy. She lives and works in Pacific Grove, California, where she enjoys morning walks, reading, and time with friends. **See chapter 1.**

Maria Gitin is the author of *This Bright Light of Ours 1965*, a memoir and oral history of the voting rights struggle in Wilcox County, Alabama, to be published in 2014. She lectures on the 1965 Voting Rights Movement and leads diversity training nationally. She lives in Capitola, California. Stories and interviews are available at her blog: http://thislittlelight1965 .wordpress.com. **See chapter 4.**

Markie Louise Christianson (L. C.) Blumer, PhD, LMFT, LMHC, is an assistant professor of family studies and family therapy at the University of Nevada, Las Vegas. In addition to serving as a longtime editorial board member of the *Journal of Feminist Family Therapy: An International Forum*, Markie has authored over thirty publications and conducted over twenty presentations and workshops in the areas of social justice practices, experiences of sexual and gender orientation minorities, mentoring and supervisory relationships, technology and clinical practice, and ecological and family sustainability. **See chapter 7.**

Molly Lewis grew up in Connecticut and Maryland. She worked in higher education for more than thirty years and is currently an administrator at

Hartnell College in Salinas, California, overseeing grant-funded programs in workforce development and technical education. Originally trained as an anthropologist and a teacher of English as a Second Language, she has traveled extensively and enjoys exploring world languages and cultures. Her weekends are busy with grandchildren, gardening, and music. **See chapter 3.**

Natasha Fraley grew up in Philadelphia, Pennsylvania, and now lives and works in Pacific Grove, California. Her work as an interpretive planner and exhibit developer for museums, aquaria, parks, and other exhibit venues necessitates traveling throughout California, as well as to far-flung places like Florida and West Virginia. Natasha practices qi gong and pilates and loves to go hiking. **See chapter 1.**

Patricia Hamilton lives and works in Pacific Grove, California, where her publishing office, Park Place Publications, is located. She writes, publishes, and distributes healthy travel guides. Since 1982, Patricia has helped others develop, self-publish, and market books in all genres. She enjoys yoga, TM (transcendental meditation), gardening, walking, and spending time with her two grandchildren. **See chapter 3.**

Paula has worked in the field of organizational transformation and leadership development for twenty-five years. She recently expanded her work to include personal transformation. She is a sought-after seminar leader, speaker, and consultant and is currently writing a book on finding individual purpose and taking action. She lives near Monterey, California, and is president of a corporation. Paula enjoys yoga, gardening, blues music, any form of dancing, and being outside in nature. **See chapter 5.**

Peter lives in Pacific Grove, California, and is the longtime owner of a successful auto collision shop. He is disturbed by social injustice and wants to always be part of solutions rather than the problems. Peter is joyous about his return to skateboarding. **See chapter 8.**

Robert Weston got his PhD in 1973, taught a while, and then moved into human resource management for hi-tech companies. He retired in 2002 and lives in Holmes Beach, Florida. He has published three books of poems and some essays and stories. He writes, teaches in the local Lifetime Learning Academy, is on the board of directors of the Breakthrough Men's Community, and is a cofounder and practitioner of Neural Somatic Integration, a somatic psychotherapy process. **See chapter 8.**

Rosi Jansson Edwards spent her early childhood in Finland and the remainder of her childhood and adolescence in New York City. A retired psychologist, she has lived in Pacific Grove, California, for many years. When Rosi and her husband, Dwight Edwards, are not traveling, they serve as chaplains for retired clergy in the El Camino Real Diocese. She also enjoys Tai Chi, opera, art museums, daily walks, and correspondence with friends. **See chapter 2.**

Sue Parris lives in Pacific Grove, California. She is regional director for the National Coalition Building Institute, a nonprofit leadership training organization, and provides consultation and training to nonprofit and public agencies, schools, and businesses. Outside of working, she enjoys cooking, being outdoors, and time with friends. **See chapter 6.**

Susan DeMersseman, PhD, is a psychologist and writer in the San Francisco Bay Area, where she has worked with children and families for more than thirty years. Her writing has appeared in many national publications and in several books. She grew up in South Dakota and has shared that experience along with the rich community of the Bay Area with her now-grown children. Her workshops and website present a humorous and touching look at raising children, gardens, and awareness. **See chapter 8.**

Susan Mehra, PhD, is a licensed clinical psychologist. She has conducted a private therapy practice in Monterey, California, for the past twenty-five years. In addition, she sings with the Carmel Bach Festival, I Cantori di Carmel, and conducts a chamber ensemble, VOCI a cappella. Music is her own form of therapy. **See chapter 4.**

Tom Foley lives in Cumberland Foreside, Maine. He is a retired sales and marketing executive who has traveled extensively in the United States and

Canada. He is an active member of his community, serving on local boards and committees. **See chapters 7 and 8.**

Valerie Kack lives in Grass Valley, California, on seven acres of forest. She has been a clinical social worker for forty years and is in private practice. She is also an artist, and her work can be seen at Kackart.com. She has published *The Emotion Handbook, For the Recovery and Management of Feelings* (1992) and *For She Is the Tree of Life, Grandmothers as Seen Through the Eyes of Women Writers* (1995). **See chapters 1, 5, and 8.**

Yolanda Gabrielle lives in Providence, Rhode Island. She has been a behavioral health therapist for fourteen years, and prior to that she was an English teacher. She enjoys gardening, traveling, the arts, and movies. **See chapter 8.**